The Extraordinary Life of an Ordinary Girl

BOOK ONE

MY FATHER'S DEMONS

ANGELA PEACOCK

PAGE PUBLISHING
Conneaut Lake, PA

First originally published by Page Publishing 2023

ISBN 979-8-88793-219-4 (pbk)
ISBN 979-8-88793-224-8 (digital)

Printed in the United States of America

To my children. When I look at you, I wonder how such perfection came from this broken and scarred vessel. I thank God with every breath that He entrusted you to me. I love you all fiercely!

Chapter 1

One of my earliest memories was around the age of five. It was the end of my first day of kindergarten, and I sat alone in the first seat of the school bus, the one behind the driver. All I could think about was getting home so that I could tell Mama and Daddy about my day.

Looking back on the days leading up to this moment, I recall being more nervous about starting school than I had ever been about anything before in my short life. Sure, I had attended preschool, but in my mind, that was just an older version of daycare. This was kindergarten, and I was officially on my way to being the "big girl" Mama always said that I was.

Together, we had done everything possible to prepare me for this day.

We'd taken our time and carefully thought about every detail, starting with my clothes. Even at this young age, I knew that what I wore would play a big part in the first impression I made on everyone. I wanted to make sure the outfit that I chose would somehow give the teacher a sense that I was a serious student and not a troublemaker. I was there to be a sponge and soak up all the knowledge that she was willing to pour into me. On the other hand, I did not want to come across to the other children as though I were a know-it-all or aiming to become the teacher's pet. There was a fine line I needed to walk, and I had found just the right outfit to help me do that.

Next on the list? How to wear my hair. It must convey that I was serious about my education, yet I was not above playing on the merry-go-round or swinging upside down on the monkey bars. Not knowing if recess would be at the beginning, end, or somewhere in the middle of my day meant I had to choose a style that would allow for maximum play without leaving me looking like a ragamuffin. There was only one choice I could think of that would meet the requirements of my kindergarten debut.

With my hairstyle chosen, it was time to plan what I would take for lunch. I couldn't eat anything that might make me sick as I was already battling nerves in anticipation of the biggest day of my life. I settled on a safe, reliable favorite, put it in my new lunch box, and packed it away in the refrigerator.

It was the night before school started. With each detail I could think of completed, I brushed my teeth, kissed Mama and Daddy good night, and went to bed. I woke up the next morning full of excitement. Finally, the day I'd spent so much time and energy obsessing over was here.

I found my clothes at the foot of my bed, where Mama had laid them. As I put them on, a sense of calm and comfort overwhelmed me. "Aah!" They were still warm from the ironing she'd given them. Beside my clothes were the shoes we'd purchased just the day before. Even though they were new, I could see they were damp from the unnecessary wipe down Mama had given them. If fussing over small and insignificant details made her feel like a better mother, then so be it. I wasn't about to ruin the moment for her. I knew she was the best mama in the entire world, and whatever it took for her to believe it was fine with me.

I quickly put on my socks and shoes. I knew Daddy was waiting to help me complete the next step in my preparations.

I rounded the corner into the bathroom, where Daddy was waiting to inspect my teeth once I brushed them. He motioned for me to assume the "ahh" position. As the obedient child that I am, I opened my mouth as big and wide as I could. Using a flashlight, he peeked inside to inspect for any traces of last night's dinner that may have lingered. Once satisfied that there were no stragglers, he told me to blow out my breath as hard as I could. He wanted to make sure my breath wouldn't chase people away.

After passing all of his tests for cleanliness, we moved on to the task of turning my built-in mop into hair. Mama swore it was a rat's nest, and staring at my reflection in the mirror this morning, I thought she might be right, but Daddy started brushing the tangles away, and before long, my hair was smooth and silky. Now tamed, he tied it back with a red velvet ribbon.

Meanwhile, Mama quickly readied my baby sister for the adventure of taking me to school on my first day of kindergarten. I watched as she poured a bottle of milk and set it in a bowl of hot water to take the chill off. While the bottle was warming, Mama grabbed a handful of diapers and a pacifier. She stuffed them into a diaper bag before returning to the bed where Tracy was sleeping. With a soothing, gentle touch, Mama rolled Tracy onto her back and quickly changed her diaper. Now that she was powdered and changed, Mama wrapped Tracy in a blanket and scooped her up. Tracy simply stretched, rolled her eyes, and snuggled into Mama's arms, falling back to sleep. With Tracy resting comfortably in her arms, seemingly undisturbed, Mama removed the bottle from the bowl of water and signaled she was ready.

Daddy grabbed the car keys off the coffee table and opened the door while motioning with his hand for us to exit. "Ladies, after you."

My lunch box in hand, pencils, crayons, and extra paper neatly loaded into the backpack I carried on my shoulders, I walked out ready for the vast unknown world of big kids' school.

The only thing left to do was to get there! I knew after today, I would be riding the bus to and from school, but this was my first day, and my parents wanted to make it special, so they drove me to school. Thinking about it now from a parent's perspective, I am certain the real motive for driving me that first morning had more to do with the realization that I was growing up and it was time for them to start letting go, rather than the pretense of walking me to class so they could help me settle in for the day.

The closer we got to school, the more nervous I became, and it was obvious to my parents. They kept reassuring me that the butterflies swarming around my stomach would go away. At some point in my day, I would be so caught up in meeting new people and learning new things that I wouldn't even remember the moment they left.

They were right. The nerves I battled for days went away almost immediately when the teacher, Mrs. Holbrook, smiled at me for the first time. She had short, gray, curly hair like Granny's, and a warm, welcoming smile also like hers. Mrs. Holbrook was shorter than I expected and maybe even a little older than I had imagined, but she was so much nicer than I ever dreamed.

She must have sensed my nerves because she knew exactly what to do. Mrs. Holbrook sat me next to another shy, nervous girl who would become my best friend over the course of that year in kindergarten. I can no longer remember the girl's name, but I will never forget all of the time we spent together braiding blades of grass and pine needles into bracelets, crowns, necklaces, and any other accessory we could think of. We talked about which boys we thought were cute and which ones were gross. We traded scratch and sniff stickers, which by the end of the year covered our lunch boxes. We laughed at everything and at nothing. We were simply two little girls who needed each other in order to navigate the uncharted waters of our first year in the big kids' world of elementary school, and it all started on this day.

Before I knew it, my first day of kindergarten was over.

I made it! As I sat on the bus thinking about my day, I smiled. Awkward first meetings, breakfast in the huge cafeteria filled with kids, coloring, recess, lunch, and a nap, I'd done it all, and I'd made it! It was a full and busy day, but I made it!

So many things happened that first day of kindergarten, and I could have been distracted with thoughts of any one of them.

Even sitting on the bus, waiting to go home had its temptations for me to be distracted, like the two boys who sat in the seat beside me. I suspected they were brothers by the way they were dressed, along with the matching red hair and freckles they were both adorned with. Each of them wore a shirt with a character from Winnie the

Pooh. They even sported the same black tennis shoes with a thin white line from toe to heel.

The boys were playing with a lizard rescued by the one who wore an orange Tigger shirt and brown pants. Moments before, the lizard had been in the bus aisle just as a recently released herd of school kids were about to get on. The boys almost cracked their heads with one another as they each hurried to snatch up the lizard from what was sure to be his untimely death. Thankful for their quick action, I could now see that the lizard was safe as it perched between the eyes of Eeyore on the second boy's shirt.

Relieved, I turned to see the back of the bus driver's head. It was bobbing just out of time with every bump in the road. I smiled. The motion reminded me of the doll glued to the dashboard of my cousin's car. It was some sort of tourist trinket intended to make people think he'd been to some tropical destination, but the tchotchke didn't fool those of us who knew he bought it at a yard sale. Still, she danced on his dash in a grass hula skirt and flower lei, bobbing her head and swinging her hips, bidding anyone who looked long enough to come away with her. At times, I thought I heard the sound of waves crashing on the shore as I watched her sway back and forth.

I could have gotten lost in any one of these distractions.

I didn't.

All I could think of was how proud I was going to make Mama and Daddy when I told them about my first day of school. I'd made new friends, had fun at recess, and had done all of the things they said I would, but what was going to make them most proud was what Mrs. Holbrook said. She told me how smart, quiet, and respectful I was. She also said that I followed instructions perfectly. Mrs. Holbrook even gave me a gold star to wear on my shirt. I glanced down to make sure it was still there. I didn't want to lose it before they'd had a chance to see it. I was excited in anticipation of their reaction when the bus rounded the corner onto the road where I lived and stopped in front of my house.

The house was old and white with a black shingled roof. It had two windows, one on either side of the door. Each window was bordered by black shutters that were only there for looks as neither set actually closed. The steps that led to the door had scrolling wrought-iron posts on each side. They were also painted black. On the steps in front of the door was a green welcome mat that resembled fake grass. It had a dual purpose. The first was to extend an invitation to all to come inside. The second was to provide a place to wipe one's feet. The message was clear, "You are welcome here, as long as you clean the dirt off your shoes first!"

The small house was located at the back of the lot on which it sat. The lot could not have been more than a quarter acre in size. I remember every time it rained, the yard would flood due to the slope of the ground that led away from the road, down a small hill to the house. The puddles that were left by the rain seemed to call my name, beckoning me to come and play. Daddy was adamant! I was not allowed outside or anywhere near the puddles when it rained, but Daddy had to work, and what he didn't know wouldn't hurt him.

From time to time, Mama would have errands to run or chores to do around the house. During these times, she needed help watching Tracy and me. Mama would call for my cousins to come over so they could watch us and keep us occupied while she was busy. I loved having them over. The things we did with them were so much fun and usually against the rules. They didn't care!

My cousin Denise was notorious for breaking Daddy's rules. She knew how stern my father was and that he wanted us to be clean at all times. She didn't care! In her mind, rules were meant to be broken. Every time it rained and there were puddles, Denise would sit us in the middle of them and say, "Have at it!" I remember laughing and playing, all while having the time of my life. By the end of the day, we would be covered in mud and no longer recognizable. Denise was always conscious of keeping a close eye on the clock to be sure how long we had before Daddy would return home. When it was almost time for him, she would wash us down with the water hose, which caused us to become even more rambunctious and rowdy. Once we were sufficiently free of the mud pies that covered us, she would usher us inside for a proper bath. By the time Daddy got home, we would, once again, be the perfectly clean little angels he'd left on his way out the door that morning, and he was none the wiser to our mischief.

I came to see the slope of the house as a disguise for those puddles I loved playing in so very much, hiding them from Daddy while they waited to be revealed by the rain.

Staring out of the bus window, reminiscing about the last time I played in those puddles, I noticed the large, grandfather oak trees standing guard on each side of the house. Both had branches that resembled arms, and they appeared to be reaching out to one another over the roof. I imagined each tree was stretching in an effort to embrace the other, with both being denied just short of the craved touch. There were nights when the wind would blow so hard it caused the trees to scrape against the house on every side. The noises coming from outside scared me, and I would hide under my blankets, where I occasionally dared to peek out from my refuge to see if anything was coming to get me. I came to believe the noises I heard were the trees crying out to one another, that they were as scared as I was, each one begging the other to stretch just a little further, pleading that they increase the effort to reach out for the touch that would bring much needed comfort from the storm, but nature was cruel, and no matter how hard they tried, the embrace was always denied.

Lost in the possibility of comfort among trees, I was brought back to reality when the bus stopped. As I gathered my things and prepared to get off, it was clear to me that there would be no puddles to play in on this day. If the trees were trying to console each other at the wind's behest, I don't remember. What I do remember isn't a storm that nature conjured up. It is the storm that my daddy unleashed in his fury.

Though I did not know it at the time, I can only attribute that we survived this day to the grace and protection of God. No doubt, God has been with me since before He formed me in my mother's womb. However, I believe it was at this moment when the image of my earthly father was shattered that God introduced Himself to me. He broke open the seed of Himself that He'd placed within me from the foundation of the world. Though I did not realize it at the time, this is where my journey with my heavenly Father begins.

Chapter 2

Looking back, I can see myself clearly as I stepped off the canary yellow school bus. I was wearing a thigh-length, vivid blue, polyester overall dress with big red buttons that fastened the straps. Underneath the dress was a shirt with multicolored, mix-matched patchwork designs, puffed sleeves, and a huge white collar. My long, straight, sandy blond hair was tied back in a ponytail tamed by a red velvet bow. On my feet, I was wearing the first of countless pairs of black and white saddle oxford shoes I would own throughout my adolescent life. In my left hand, I was holding a Wonder Woman lunch box that contained a half-eaten peanut butter and grape jelly sandwich, an apple core, and an empty thermos that earlier in the day held truly southern sweet tea. I can see that everything I spent so much time planning with Mama leading up to this day has been accomplished with near perfection.

As I watched this scene unfold, I couldn't help but feel the same excitement I felt then in anticipation of telling Mama and Daddy all about my day. As soon as my feet touched the ground, I took off running toward the house. That short distance from the road to the door suddenly seemed like miles.

I was almost to the steps when I heard their voices.

I could tell he was angry when he started calling her names. "Whore! Slut!"

What do those words mean?

Mama was crying and begging Daddy to stop. "Please, Skip. Please, baby. I love you. You're hurting me. Think about the girls."

In an instant, my excitement was gone, and in its place was horror. Her cries seemed to be getting softer and more strained. *What is happening? Why is mama crying? Why is Daddy so mad? And where is my baby sister?*

I need to hurry! I need to get to that door! I have to stop him!

They didn't realize that I was home until I opened the door. Fear gripped every part of me! I dropped my lunch box and started screaming, "Daddy, STOP! Please STOP! YOU'RE HURTING MAMA!"

He turned to see me standing in the doorway and immediately let go of the belt he was using to choke her. She started coughing and gasping for air. I could see the rage in his eyes turn to shame as he realized the fear he had caused in mine. I ran to Mama, and Daddy ran outside.

She was tied to one of the kitchen chairs, naked. I could see scratches and bruises covering her body. There was blood and mucus coming from her nose, and it was mingled with the blood and saliva covering her mouth. Her left eye was swollen shut and already turning purple. She was sobbing as she hung her head in shame and embarrassment. I stroked her hair, trying to console her in the same way that she consoled me any time I was hurt.

"Shhhh, it's okay, Mama. I am here, I love you, and I will make it all better."

She lifted her head and smiled. I know she was trying to be brave for me and Tracy, but she was in so much pain that it was impossible to hide.

What can I do?

That's when I noticed her hands were still tied behind her back with one of my daddy's ties. I hurried to the back of the chair and quickly worked to loosen the knot. Before long, her hands were free, and she was scooping Tracy up into her arms in an effort to soothe her cries. I rushed to the bedroom and grabbed a blanket to cover them both. I wanted the blanket to comfort Tracy, but mostly I wanted to erase the shame from my mama's face that I know came from her nakedness and vulnerability.

As I spread the blanket over them, Mama looked up and met my worried, frightened stare with a smile that told me she was going to be okay and that she was grateful for my help. I knelt down beside them and wrapped my arms around Mama's leg. As I leaned my head on her knee, she returned the comfort I gave her moments before with a run of her hand through my hair.

In that moment, the man who was the hero in my world became the man I would resent and hate for most of my life. What had he done?! Didn't he know that this was my mama? My mama!

I looked up from staring out the window at an empty driveway just in time to see the pain in her eyes—the pain that came with the recognition that I, her five-year-old daughter, have just been exposed to the monster that is my daddy.

Chapter 3

It has been two weeks since that day—the day he might have killed my mama had I not walked in. When he ran out of the door, I prayed he would never come back, but he did. It wasn't that night, thankfully.

His absence allowed the three of us to comfort one another and grieve for what was lost.

For Tracy, it was the facade of a loving father. She would never grow up to know the loving and gentle father that I once knew. Now that the puppet master had been revealed, it would never go back behind the curtain in hiding for any significant period of time.

For Mama, it was her sense of dignity that was lost. She would never recover from the shame that I saw in her eyes that day—the shame that came from being the woman who stayed in an abusive relationship.

For me? For me, it was the loss of so many things, my image of Daddy as a good and loving father, the innocence of being a naive child, and the sense of security and safety parents are supposed to provide to their children.

Every window in my young world was shattered that day, but I realized it was all built with stained glass painted with counterfeit brush strokes. Once the facade was gone, I was able to see the reality of the world in which I lived.

When Daddy finally came home, he acted as if nothing had happened. He came through the door, arms full—milk and doughnuts in one and a bouquet of flowers in the other. He was attempting to buy our forgiveness. The milk and doughnuts were for Tracy and me. The red roses were for Mama. They were her favorite, and he knew that. Even I knew that. Surely she would not fall for his cheap attempts at making up for almost killing her in front of us.

How could he not see the wreckage he left in his wrath? Did he not see the cuts and bruises on Mama's face and body? The ones left there by none other than his own hands? Didn't he notice that her eye was swollen shut? That it was bulging with black and blue pillows of blood surrounding it?

If he couldn't see what he had done to Mama, surely, he could see the fear and betrayal in my eyes.

I could see him for what he was, but apparently, Mama couldn't or wouldn't. It hadn't even been twenty-four hours since his rampage, yet here he was—back in "HIS" house, back in "HIS" recliner, back in "HIS" chair at the kitchen table, and back in "HIS" bed! It made me sick. He had not laid a hand on me in his fit, and still I was terrified at the thought of being near him. Mama, on the other hand, still had the evidence of his evil on every inch of her body, yet he was caressing and touching her as if nothing had happened. I could not wrap my mind around what was happening. No matter how hard I tried, I couldn't make any sense of it.

He spent the next two weeks doting on us. I can only assume that it was a sense of guilt that fueled his actions. He bought Mama a new dress. Of course, it was red. Once again, he knew what her favorites were, and he used them to smooth the pathway back into her heart. Tracy and I got new, matching rompers. They were the kind that included both shorts and a shirt connected at the waist with spaghetti straps tied into a bow that sat on your shoulders. The rompers were yellow with orange palm tree leaves and a white border hemmed around the legs and at the top. We wore them the next day when he took us all to Busch Gardens for the first time.

I hated myself for the excitement I was feeling. It turned out I was exactly the same as Mama—the only difference being the cost of my forgiveness—one day of magic at a theme park.

It was a wonderfully, marvelous, spectacular day! That is what my child self would say.

There were so many things to do, and I couldn't wait to get started.

We rode the train through the Savannah, where we saw elephants, gazelles, giraffes, and a number of other wild animals. We even saw a rhinoceros! The best part of the animal tour happened when we stopped by the cheetah enclosure. Mama let Tracy stand on her own with her hands pressed against the glass while we all looked at the beautiful mama cat. She didn't seem to take any notice of us, but her young cub did. None of us were paying attention when the juvenile cat pounced on the window in front of Tracy as if nudging her to come and play. I'm sure he just saw someone his own size and curiosity took over, but it scared Tracy, and she started to scream. The young cheetah ran and hid behind his mother, and our mama just picked Tracy up and pointed at the camel behind us. The distraction seemed to soothe Tracy for the moment, but the animal tour portion of our day was done. As far as Daddy and I were concerned, that was just fine. We were ready for the more adventurous things the theme park had to offer.

The thrill-seeking, adrenaline junky part of me couldn't help but notice the enormous roller coasters strategically placed throughout the park. This was one time when I was thankful to be taller than most other kids my age. I was just the right height to pass the requirements, allowing Daddy and I to ride every roller coaster they had. We took our chances on the mighty Python, the swirling Scorpion, the swinging Phoenix, and every other beast-turned roller coaster that needed taming. With each coaster, we would pick our place in line, carefully counting the number of people and carts to make sure we were the ones in either the first or the last seats. According to Daddy, everybody knew those were the best seats if you wanted to maximize the thrill of feeling your stomach flip and your head go dizzy. He was right! Each time our cart slowly climbed the track to the top of a peak, I could feel the anticipation of the coming fall build with extreme intensity in the pit of my gut. Once we reached the top, I held my breath for what I knew was coming next—unbridled speed down a hill, swirling around a curve or upside down! If ever I was addicted to anything in my life, it happened that day. I became addicted to roller coasters with my very first hill.

While Daddy and I chased our highs, Mama held Tracy by the entrance to each ride. She would coax Tracy to smile and wave each time we came flying past. I could have ridden forever, but Daddy wanted to make sure that all of us were enjoying ourselves equally. Not wanting to be selfish, I reluctantly agreed to end our solo coaster riding for the day when Daddy found a ride that we could all go on together.

It was the white-water rapids. Mama was allowed to hold Tracy in her lap while she sat between Daddy and me. Once we were strapped in, the operator launched the raft. Off we went! It didn't take long for this to become my favorite ride. The raft would spin in circles while navigating the rocky and wet rapids. From time to time, we would bump into a large boulder, which caused the raft to change directions and jerk its occupants from side to side and up and then down. Meanwhile, the river rewarded our maneuvers by spraying torrential amounts of water on all of us. We were soaked by the time the ride was over, but we could not have cared less. It was so much fun that we rode it over and over, again and again. It took hours for the withered effect the water had on my hands and feet to disappear.

As much fun as the rapids had been, there was no way that Daddy was going to allow us to get in his car while we were wet. To remedy the situation, we walked around the main street area of the park, where we took in the dolphin show, a falconry display, and a magical cobra dance.

I remember being drawn in by the music. It was mesmerizing. Apparently, my parents thought so too because we all stopped to watch the show. The music was coming from a man who played a wooden flute while he sat behind a woven wicker basket that was covered with a lid. The man was dressed in ancient Moroccan attire consisting of puffy, shiny blue and gold pants and a purple shirt overlaid with a shimmering multicolored vest that was only half the length of a traditional vest. On his head was a red turban that had a large yellow gemstone fastened to the front. To me, he looked like a genie right out of a movie.

On the left side of the stage was a beautiful woman with long, raven-black hair and green eyes. They were intensified by the way she wore her makeup. She was dressed as a belly dancer with a matching top and bottoms. Both were made out of sheer, royal blue fabric with sequins and tassels of emerald green and gold throughout the ensemble, further intensifying the green in her eyes. The top stopped snugly under her breasts, leaving her belly button exposed and adorned with a diamond to catch the light as she moved. When the music started, she began her dance. Slowly, she swayed her hips from side to side while the man played his flute. All of a sudden, we watched in awe as a cobra began to emerge from the basket, weaving back and forth with the same rhythm and motion as the woman.

I was amazed, but Tracy was entranced! It was as if she was hypnotized by the performance in the same way the snake was. She couldn't take her eyes off the stage. Daddy had been carrying her to give Mama a rest, and now he put her on his shoulders, allowing her a better view of the stage. After watching the show several times, we finally tore ourselves away, with Tracy screaming for more. The promise of food and ice cream seemed to be the only thing that would pacify her at that moment.

Knowing her silence wouldn't last long, we followed our noses and found a food court not far from where we were. The choices seemed endless. There was something for everyone, no matter what you craved. Whether you wanted a pizza, a smoked turkey leg, or hamburgers, you could have it. I settled on a hot dog with French fries and a coke. Once we finished our lunch, Daddy bought us ice cream, just as he'd promised. We scarfed it down in mere minutes and were onto the next adventure.

By the time we left Busch Gardens, we had eaten all sorts of food, played silly games for prizes, watched all kinds of shows, seen more varieties of animals than I even knew existed, and ridden everything. We were exhausted. As we carried our haul of stuffed giraffes and hippos back to the car, I stared up at my father and smiled. I believed, in that moment, that I had my daddy back. The monster was gone.

On the way home, my belief that the monster was gone was reinforced when Daddy finally apologized to Mama. Tracy was fast asleep, and I was starting to doze off. I'm sure he thought I was already asleep and would not hear him when he reached out to touch Mama's hair and said, "Baby, I am so sorry for what I did. I don't know what happened, but I promise it will NEVER happen again. Do you hear me? NEVER! Please forgive me. Will you forgive me?" My mama simply leaned her head into his hand and nodded. He was apologizing and promising to never hurt her again. Surely he meant it; after all, he had just given us the best day of our lives. A monster wouldn't do that, so Daddy had to be back. With that, I laid my head down on the seat and closed my eyes. I silently prayed to Jesus and thanked Him for bringing back my daddy. Finally, this nightmare was over, wasn't it? I could forgive him too, couldn't I?

Chapter 4

That night, I dreamed of riding roller coasters. It was sort of like the times we visited the beach. I would play in the waves the entire day, letting them carry me onto the shore and back out into the ocean just to the point where I could barely touch the sandy bottom if I stood on my tiptoes. At night, when it was time to go to bed, I could feel the tug and pull of the ocean as if I was still riding those waves. That was how this felt. The knots I felt in my stomach now were the same ones that I felt each time our cart would start to descend a steep hill or go around a loop superfast. I never wanted to wake up. This dream was the best!

Reality came with Mama's gentle touch that she used to wake me. I tried hanging on to sleep as long as I could, knowing that with its departure would go the last crumbs of the delicious adventure I had devoured the day before.

Mama was not going to allow me to relish in the remnants of my dream any longer, so I reluctantly opened my eyes and snarled at her. She returned my greeting with a happy and mischievous smile that reminded me of the Cheshire Cat from Alice in Wonderland. Mama was definitely up to something. She had already laid out my clothes for the day. I looked over to where she was directing my attention, and she said, "You need to hurry and get dressed. Breakfast is waiting."

The natural sleuth in me kicked in. I tried to figure out what she was up to and where we were going by the clothes she had set out. It was one of my better T-shirts—a red one with white letters that said, "Shazam!" Folded underneath was a pair of faded blue denim shorts I had only worn a few times. This meant that whatever the plans were, she wanted me to look nice but still be comfortable enough to play.

Still grasping for the wisps on the tail end of my dream about yesterday, a hope started to take shape. Was it possible that we were going back to Busch Gardens?! Yesterday had been so much fun, and maybe they decided they were not ready for it to be over either.

I hurried to put on my clothes. I started to brush my hair, but when I looked in the mirror, I could see it didn't need it. The French braid Mama put in last night, before I went to bed, was still holding strong. The last thing I needed to do was put on my socks and shoes. I chose my favorite pair of sneakers and a pair of socks that were white with little red pom-poms hanging off the back. I was ready.

When I rounded the corner into the kitchen, I could already smell that Mama had made my favorites for breakfast. Sure enough, there sat a bowl of tomato gravy, with a biscuit on the saucer under-neath. Both were still hot enough that I could see the steam rising from them. Mama cut my biscuit in half and slathered butter on both sides before putting them back together. My mouth started to water as I watched the butter ooze out of the biscuit and onto the saucer. Daddy was standing at the stove, tending to what would be his contribution to this morning's feast, a cast-iron frying pan full of crispy bacon! He brought the searing hot pan to the table, careful to protect his hand by covering it with an oven mitt. Mama reached in and brought back a handful of bacon that she dropped on the edge of my saucer.

I sat down in the chair, folded my hands, and thanked Jesus for being so good to me. He had given me the best day ever. He let me dream about all of the fun I'd had that day. He made Mama fix my favorite breakfast, and best of all, He fixed my daddy. How could anybody not love Jesus?

As I sat there eating, I thought of the stories told to me about Jesus and His love for me, stories I'd heard in Sunday school, from

Mama, and especially from Granny. This must be what it felt like to be loved by Him—a love so strong that even the small things, the things that seem insignificant to others, matter to Him because they matter to me.

I ate an entire bowl of gravy, all of my bacon, and at least two biscuits—not to mention I drank enough orange juice to float a boat. All the while, I kept thinking about the love I was feeling as I sat there. I knew that my parents loved me, and I knew that my grandparents loved me. This was something different. I could not see where the love was coming from. I could not tell you specifically what caused me to feel this love. All I knew was what I felt inside. This love was never going to leave me. It would be there, good, bad, or otherwise. This love came from the one they said died for me. I had no idea just how much I needed Him, but He knew. Thank God, He knew.

Brought back from my thoughts by the sound of Tracy hiccupping, I finished my breakfast, placed my dishes in the sink, grabbed her diaper bag, and headed out the door. I climbed into the backseat of Daddy's prized 1965 Ford Mustang. It was metal-flaked, midnight blue, with black leather seats that were always scorching hot from the Florida sun, no matter what time of year it was. The car was immaculate! There wasn't a scratch on it or a tear in it, and Daddy was adamant that he was going to keep it that way. He washed and polished it weekly, which included wiping the inside down and sweeping the floorboards with a small hand broom. It took him hours, but Daddy loved that car, and I did too.

As we left that day, Mama sat in the front passenger seat, holding Tracy in her lap. As usual, I took my position in the back, right in the middle of the bench seat, so I could peek through the opening between the front two seats. I wanted to see Daddy shift the gears in response to the engine when it roared for his attention. I was amazed that he could control the creature with a mere touch of his hands and a shift of his feet, but then again, my daddy was a god when I was that age. There was nothing he couldn't do.

Watching his hands, I couldn't help being transported back to the day I saw those same hands around my mama's tiny neck. He was very big at six feet, two inches tall and weighting two hundred seventy pounds. She was a stark contrast at five feet, four inches, and all of one hundred and fifteen pounds, soaking wet. It is said that opposites attract, and in the case of my parents, that could not have been more true.

Both were striking at this age.

He had chiseled Viking good looks with silky blond hair and piercing, ice blue eyes—a true mixture of his Irish and Dutch ancestors.

She was beautiful, with Native American heritage gifted to her from her father, mingled with German from her mother's side. She had chestnut brown eyes and hair that matched. It flowed past her shoulders, touching the middle of her back. Her tanned face was sprinkled with freckles that she tried to hide with makeup whenever we would go out, though I never understood why. I loved her freckles and always wanted some for myself.

In the days that passed since the first time I'd found my father beating my mother, I tried to reconcile, in my young mind, how Daddy could have ever done such a thing. That was not my daddy. My daddy loved her. He protected her. He doted on her.

Truth be told, he doted on all of us. He always made sure to tell each of us how much he wanted and cherished us. He took time out of his days to interact and play with us.

There wasn't much Daddy wouldn't do to make Tracy and me smile. He made silly faces and sounds, trying to coax a laugh out of us. When we did allow a laugh to escape, he would seize the opportunity to hold us down and tickle us; of course, we would laugh even harder. Looking back now, these are the times I long for when I think about my father, those days when Daddy was my hero, when Daddy was my safe place, the one I ran to for shelter.

The three of us spent most days simply being with one another and enjoying our time together, laughing and cutting up, always seeing who could play the best tricks on the others. Once the shenanigans we found ourselves in were over, Tracy and I would get our baths and brush our teeth. Tracy didn't have very many teeth, but she seemed to enjoy standing at attention in the same way that I did, waiting for the routine inspection Daddy gave to ensure proper oral hygiene.

From time to time, Mama would ask Daddy to comb my hair while she dressed Tracy for bed, and he would sing to me the whole time, "Don't know much about history, don't know biology, but I know that I love you."

Daddy had a great voice, and he knew it. Anyone who heard him sing would tell him that he sounded like Elvis, which only served to inflate his ego even more than it already was. He relished the attention. What those people didn't know about him was the side I'd witnessed that horrific day.

I couldn't help but wonder if he would have killed Mama had I not walked in. That is when I realized, no matter how sweet and loving he seemed to be, there had been a monster living inside of him. Was it still there? Was it lurking just underneath the surface waiting for the opportunity to finish what it started? The monster's existence meant that Daddy could never again be fully trusted. He could never again be a god to me. I now knew that he had never really been a god.

God was the love that I felt at breakfast, the love that I still felt warming my heart. Thinking that Daddy was a god was simply a side effect of being blinded by those stained-glass windows I saw my life through, but they were forever shattered. I now realize there is only one God, and His love cannot be replaced or imitated by any other.

I was lost in my thoughts when I heard a commotion break out in the front seat. We were stopped at a four-way stop sign, and I heard my father in a rage. He was ranting and raving to my mother, accusing the man at the stop sign to our right of staring at Mama. Surely, the man must have seen that he was in the car with her, according to Daddy. That meant the man was blatantly disrespecting Daddy. There was no way he was going to get away with that.

The presumed guilty guy was driving what I would come to know later in life as a brown Ford Pinto. It looked as if it was new, evidenced by the paper tag taped in the hatchback window.

The man proceeded through his stop-sign first. Then it was our turn. My father slammed his foot down on the gas pedal, causing the tires to scream in anticipation of what was about to happen. My sister fell back against Mama in response to the sudden and unexpected force of gravity. This startled Tracy, causing her to launch into a hysterical outburst of screams. Mama was trying to soothe her while, at the same time, begging Daddy not to do anything crazy. "Please, Skip, it was nothing. He was simply looking both ways for traffic. Please!" Her cries never registered with him as I could see the demons had already taken control of my father. Once again, the puppeteer was moving the strings of his puppet to garner maximum impact on his vessel.

We were inches from the man's car, and Daddy was lying on the horn, swerving all over the road, leaning out of his window, and yelling for the man to pull over.

He did!

I was pleading with the man in my mind not to get out of the car. "Please! Just take off!"

The man wasn't listening.

He opened his door and got out of the car, so did my daddy, followed by Mama as she sat Tracy down in the seat she had just vacated.

Tracy was crying so hard that there were moments when she held her breath and I thought she was going to pass out, but then she would exhale, inhale, and repeat the pattern. With renewed confidence that Tracy would be fine, I turned my attention back to the scene outside the car.

The man couldn't have been more than twenty to twenty-five years old. He was handsome, with blond hair that fell around his smooth, tanned face. It just barely dared to dip and touch his shoulders. He wasn't too small or too big, but he looked as though he could hold his own if the need should arise. He was wearing a T-shirt with white, yellow, and brown horizontal stripes and a pair of tight-fitting faded blue jeans that flared at the bottom, just barely revealing white sneakers. Though I have never seen the man before or since, over the years, I have imagined him as a surfer with the beauty that only comes from being kissed by the sun.

The look of confusion that was on the man's face told me he had no clue who we were or what was going on. My father reached the spot where the man stood at the back of his car. Without any word of explanation, he slammed the man against the hatchback of the Pinto and started punching him in the face. Mama was hanging onto Daddy's arm, begging him to stop and trying to pull him away, but she couldn't. She was so tiny, and Daddy was so big. It was like watching someone try to push a mighty redwood tree down with their hands when a bulldozer is needed. Her efforts had no effect on him.

Blow after blow, it didn't take long before the poor man was covered in blood. At the sight of it, I started screaming along with Tracy. At the moment Daddy heard me, the demons faltered. I saw the shock of recognition on my father's face. It was the realization of what he had just subjected his prized possessions to. He allowed his puppet master to take over in the presence of his daughters, and for what? Because he thought the man was looking at his wife? The man could have been admiring the beautiful car or simply been looking both ways to ensure he wouldn't be pulling out into oncoming traffic as Mama had argued. Who knew? Regardless, the man certainly did nothing to deserve the beating he took.

With that realization, Daddy picked the man up, sat him on his feet, and in a deafening silence helped him to his car. Once the man was securely inside, Daddy shut the door and reached for the wallet he kept in the back pocket of his pants. I watched as my father slipped a wad of money into his victim's hand and waited for the man to drive off.

I can't remember where we were going that day, but I know that we never made it. My father and mother returned to our car, and we drove home in a silence that would not be broken even by Tracy's cries as she had fallen asleep. My father never spoke about the brutality he committed that day, but then again, he never spoke about any of the evil within him, but I will.

Chapter 5

That night, I barely slept. Every time I closed my eyes, I could see the bloody face of the man Daddy had beaten. My head was filled with the sound of Tracy's screams and Mama's pleas for Daddy to "stop!" I had been shaken to the core of who I was. As I lay there in my bed, scared and confused, I began to feel a peace that I now know can only come from God as He wrapped me in His arms and brought comfort to my broken heart.

This was the night that I exchanged the false image I had of my earthly father for the very real, unwavering love of my heavenly Father. The tug on my heart grew stronger and stronger until I could no longer ignore His knock beckoning to come in. I threw off my covers and slipped out of my bed, which now turned into an altar. I knelt as I had done so many times before with Mama as we said our prayers before going to sleep. But this time, Mama wasn't there. It was just me and the god I had been feeling pull me to Him, the god that Granny said she and Mama had given me to before I was ever born, the god that I heard died for me, the god that loved me so much that He would never hurt me or leave me. Even at this young age, I knew that I wanted this love to always be mine. And with that, I asked Jesus to save me and come live inside my heart, even though I had a sneaking suspicion He already had.

The next morning, I woke up tired but with a peace that seemed to defy the circumstances of all that I had been through. I was still basking in the experience of salvation I'd had alone in my bedroom the night before. I couldn't wait to tell Mama all about it. I wanted to share Jesus with everyone. When I rounded the corner and stepped into the living room, I could see my father's suitcases were packed and waiting by the door.

My parents were sitting at the kitchen table while Tracy was playing on the floor beside Mama. The conversation must have been very intense because neither Mama nor Daddy noticed the half-eaten cricket sticking out of Tracy's mouth. Immediately getting sick to my stomach from the sight of it, my reaction got their attention, "Ooh, that's gross! I think I am gonna be sick!" They looked down to see what was turning my face a lovely shade of gray and found Tracy, with her "snack," smiling up at them. Mama picked her up and pried Tracy's mouth open. I watched with disgust as Mama stuck her finger down Tracy's throat to see if she could dislodge what was left of the cricket.

Of course, Tracy started to cry, and Daddy started yelling at her to stop, which only made her scream louder. My father snatched Tracy from Mama's embrace and hit her diapered bottom hard enough for her to scream bloody murder. Daddy shoved Tracy back into Mama's arms and demanded, "Do something to make her stop!" Mama gave Tracy a bottle and gently started to rock back and forth, back and forth. Tracy stopped crying and started to nod off. My parents' conversation was apparently over because neither of them said another word. My father simply picked up his luggage and walked outside.

Once my sister had completely given in to the sleep that came for her, Mama gently stood and walked to the car, trying not to wake Tracy. I followed, opening the door for Mama so she could easily lay her on the car's back seat, wrapped in her favorite Big Bird blanket.

Tracy loved Big Bird. Who am I kidding? She was obsessed with everything about Sesame Street. It was one of the many disagreements we would have throughout our lives as sisters. I just didn't see the attraction to it. I would much rather watch *The Flintstones* or *Shazam!*, but Tracy was the baby and always got what she wanted, if for no other reason but to keep her from crying.

Thankfully, she wasn't crying now. Hopefully she would stay asleep during this trip to wherever we were taking Daddy.

Daddy had already loaded his suitcases into the trunk, started the car, and was waiting to leave. I climbed in beside Tracy and behind Mama, no longer caring to watch Daddy shift the gears or tame the beast under the hood of the car. I had seen real demons in him. That had been enough beast-watching for a lifetime. I never wanted to watch him do anything again except leave and never come back.

Before the cricket fiasco at breakfast, I heard my parents talking. Daddy claimed to be leaving on a business trip. I can't remember where he said he was going, but it did not matter. All that mattered was that he was leaving. He would be out of our lives. I did not know how long he would be gone, but however long we would be safe.

I listened to the radio all the way to the airport with cautious optimism. Maybe Daddy's departure was God's way of protecting us now that I had asked Jesus to live in my heart. Maybe all of the bad things were over. Surely, Jesus was making Daddy leave so he wouldn't hurt Mama again. Cautiously optimistic that my life was going to be better, I let myself get lost in the music. I saw it as a sign of hope that the happiness I longed for was coming. Happiness brought about by the safety of knowing he was on one of those airplanes and in the sky, being taken far away from us.

Suddenly, the music stopped along with the purr of the engine. I looked up, brought back from the place my thoughts had taken me, to see we'd arrived at the airport. No one dared speak. It was as if we were all playing the quiet game, except the consequence of being the first one to talk could be deadly. The only noise had been the radio playing those old fifties songs my daddy loved to sing along with, but now even the radio was silent. It was fear that kept Mama, Tracy, and me quiet, but I wasn't sure where Daddy's silence came from. Maybe it was guilt or shame for the things he'd done. Or maybe he was just lost in thought. Whatever the reason, I was thankful for it.

I watched as my father got out of the driver's seat and walked around to the back of the car. He opened the trunk lid, which allowed me to see out the rear window through the cracks the opening made. He had packed three suitcases. THREE! That meant this would be an extended trip. On previous trips, he took one large suitcase and a shaving bag. In most of those trips, he returned within a week. Surely, three suitcases along with his shaving bag meant that he was leaving forever, didn't it?

Looking through the glass at my father, I did not understand how I could love him so much that, even now, after everything he had done, there was a part of me that wanted so badly for him to stay. That feeling made me angry with myself. I hated feeling any love for him, yet here it was, swelling up in my heart and filling my eyes with tears. I was going to miss him. As badly as I wanted him gone and I wanted us to be safe from him, I was going to miss him. It was the first time in my life that I felt guilt—guilt for wanting him to leave and never come back, guilt for wanting him to stay knowing that he would inevitably lose his temper again and take it out on Mama, guilt for loving him.

Pushing my feelings for him aside, I thought about the marks I saw on Mama that morning, and I mustered up all the courage I could find within myself, and I began praying. It wasn't the bedtime prayer that I had been taught, "*Now I lay me down to sleep. I pray the Lord my soul to keep. If I should die before I wake, I pray the Lord my soul to take. Amen.*" No. Aside from my prayer for salvation the night before, this was the first real, sincere, unrehearsed prayer that I had ever prayed. As I stared at those puke-green metal suitcases, I hoped they were full of everything he needed to anchor and sustain him somewhere far away.

I closed my eyes and pleaded, "Jesus, please cause my daddy to forget about us. I am afraid he is going to kill one of us if he doesn't stay away. I don't want him to hurt anyone else, but please let him find a new family, one that will make him happy all of the time and let him stay with them." HE DID! Well, sort of.

Chapter 6

The drive home from the airport was a stark difference in comparison to the drive there. The silence that dared us to defy it boarded the airplane with my father. Now, Mama, Tracy, and I were on our way home, WITHOUT HIM! The silence was gone, as if banished from our realm! The windows were down. The radio was on with the station changed and now blaring southern gospel music with Mama singing along. She let me sit up front with Tracy still sleeping in the back.

I couldn't take my eyes off my mama. She was beautiful. I am sure that every child thinks that their mother is the most beautiful of all mothers. That is part of the built-in, magical filter God equips each child's eyes with. However, in my case, my mama was the most beautiful woman I had ever seen. I can close my eyes to this day and see her as though she were starring in a film placed at the forefront of my mind. Her hair, with its rich Cherokee heritage, was being untamed and tangled as she drove us home. Not even the wind could resist running his fingers through it. Her dark complexion was sprayed with freckles across the bridge of her nose and onto her cheeks. Each one was placed perfectly as if in response to an angel's kiss. Then there were her eyes, so warm and full of love for her children, for my sister and for me. I have never known eyes that could be so dark, yet glow and radiate with affection. Mama's beauty could make the mythical Aphrodite blush with envy.

As I stared at her, she would look over at me from time to time and smile as though every word she sang was just for me, and I knew that it was. We had a special bond. I was the oldest. She depended on me. At the same time, she trusted me with things she could not tell anyone else. In hindsight, I'm sure that our bond was strengthened by the real-life nightmares we lived through together, clinging to each other more tightly because of our shared trauma. Whatever the reason, Mama was my world. There was no pedestal too tall for her in my opinion. She deserved to laugh and be playful, especially after everything she had suffered at my father's hands.

When she turned the radio down, my stomach twisted inside me. I knew she wanted to talk about the things I had witnessed over the past few weeks, things that I had tried so hard to erase from my mind. She started with an apology—AN APOLOGY?! Why did she apologize for what my father did to her? For what HE did to the man in the car?

I tried to tell her, "Mama, it wasn't your fault," but she wouldn't listen. She was ashamed that she hadn't left him, but she was also afraid of what he might have done had she tried.

It was at that moment, at five-and-a-half years old, that she first told me why she was too scared to leave my father. Over the years, I have heard the story many times, but I only really needed to hear it once for it to be branded into the fabric of who I am.

Chapter 7

Before I tell you that story, it is imperative that I give you a little background on my upbringing and my roots in the Pentecostal faith.

My paternal grandparents were James W. Wilkins Sr. and Mabel Darlene Wilkins, better known as Jim and Darlene to their friends. To me, they were Papa and Nana, my father's parents. They had two sons, my daddy, James W. Wilkins Jr. (Skip), and my uncle Wayne. They also raised my father's two oldest children, Terry Scott and Michael Anthony. They were from my father's marriage to a woman named Linda. Neither Daddy nor Linda was capable of properly raising children when my brothers were young, so my grandparents happily took them in.

To say that Papa and Nana were Pentecostal would be a gross understatement. Over the course of his life, Papa was a tent evangelist, preacher, teacher, and the pastor of many churches. The contributions he made to the Pentecostal faith garnered him an honorary doctorate in theology. Nana was not only his loving and devoted wife but also the best Christian organist far and wide.

Together, they were unstoppable. There was no one my grandfather would not talk to about the love and salvation of Jesus. Whether it was to hardened bikers in the heart of Baltimore or Voodoo doctors that controlled the villages of Haiti, they preached the Gospel of Christ to anyone who would listen.

They ministered all over the world and even started missions and schools in Haiti. When rebels came and burned the schools down after killing some of the teachers and volunteers, Papa refused to be deterred. He built it back bigger and better than before, while honoring those lost to the violence by dedicating the schools in their names. I can't remember Papa ever being afraid of anything. He is the one who instilled in me the foundations of a faith that is just crazy enough to believe that God is in control, that He can do ANYTHING!

I recall one story in particular that he told about the miracles God performed for the Haitian people in the midst of a drought. According to Papa, he had unknowingly set up his tent across the road from a high-ranking voodoo priest. Throughout his time there, Papa would receive threats demanding that he leave. Otherwise, he would be hurt or, worse, killed. If you knew Papa, then you would know that threats only fueled him to preach harder and longer. He was definitely not a man who was easily intimidated.

Papa kept preaching, and each night of the revival, the villagers were coming out in larger groups than the previous nights. With the growing crowds, Papa was certain it was only a matter of time before he would see people flock to the altar in response to the drawing of the Holy Spirit. To his disappointment, night after night, none of the people responded when Papa gave the invitation to come and pray the prayer of salvation at the end of service.

It was the last night of the revival. The drought in Haiti was severe, both in natural terms and in spiritual terms. The people were unable to grow crops, which made food very scarce. Papa watched the voodoo priest perform ceremonial dances day in and day out, claiming he could put an end to the drought and the people's hunger. His efforts were futile and never produced a single drop of rain.

The spiritual drought was just as bad in Papa's mind. This land was cursed because the people did not serve the one, true living God. Papa knew that God was calling these people to Himself. He wanted them to know His love, His forgiveness, and His power. Papa's heart was breaking for them. He knew that God was the answer they were looking for. They would not find it in the dance of the voodoo doctor or any other god.

Papa opened the service that night the same as he had every other night, with prayer. He then turned things over to the singers and musicians while he stepped off to the side of the platform. Papa watched as the people raised their hands and danced to the music, all the while staying in their seats. He could tell the power of God was present. It was the strongest he had felt during this revival.

When the music was finished and it was time for Papa to preach, before stepping out in front of the crowd, Papa prayed, asking God if He would "Show these people who You really are and what You can do for them if they only believe." After praying, Papa remembered taking his place at the podium and starting the sermon he prepared, but then the Holy Ghost took over.

He described the moment as one of those times when you open your mouth and something comes out that you had no intention of saying. You wish with everything in you that you could reach out, grab the words, and pull them back in, but you can't. The damage is done! What had he said? While preaching his sermon, without skipping a beat, the words that came out of Papa's mouth, but were not his? "God said that if you will give your hearts to Him this night, He will send the rain, and you will ALL go to bed with your bellies full." WHAT?!

Before Papa could figure out a way to retract his statement, the people were flocking to the altars. They were worshiping. They were praising. They had their hands raised in surrender to the God that Papa had preached about for weeks. He knew that the words that came out of his mouth weren't his, so he did the only thing he knew how to do. He trusted that his God would do exactly what He said He would do. His heart full of faith and devotion, Papa thanked God for the miracle He was going to perform, even if he did not know how.

One by one, Papa started praying for the multitude that had come to the altar for salvation at the bidding of God Himself. As he neared the end of the line, Papa recalled feeling a lot like Elijah when he told the people that God would send the rain. Nana must have sensed his nerves because she started playing the organ to which the people started dancing in the Spirit with their hands and hearts lifted to the Almighty God. At just about the same time the people started dancing, a cloud formed over the area, and it started to rain.

Papa started laughing and said, "Okay, Father, I feel the rain, but how are you planning on feeding these people?" That is when Papa watched the rain fill a crack in the ground that had been left by the drought. Out of the crack climbed the biggest crab that he had ever seen. One crab! One crab! They took that crab and put it in a pot that was made out of a fifty-five-gallon drum. Some men lifted the make-shift pot and sat it on top of a fire. It was filled with water and all kinds of seasonings. Before long, the contents of the pot were boiling, and the crab was added.

There was enough crab soup to feed the entire village.

The real miracle was the voodoo priest. He was watching everything from across the road. Papa looked up from serving soup to see the man who had been his biggest obstacle, now standing before him with tears running down his face, asking for salvation. It was right there, standing at the crab pot, that Papa led the former voodoo priest to salvation through Jesus Christ.

I will never forget this miraculous story Papa told me. It was just one of many others, but the beauty of God's love for the people, Papa, and even the voodoo priest shines through so brightly to me in how He provided both naturally and spiritually that day. These are the characteristics of the God that I was beginning to know and love.

Chapter 8

As with my paternal grandparents, I was blessed with maternal grandparents who were devout Christians. My maternal grandparents were Bunnie Lee and Nellie Merline Lee. They started their marriage as poor sharecroppers who worked the cotton fields of Dothan, Alabama, along with their eight children, two boys and six girls. My mother was second to the youngest. All of their children, with the exception of the youngest, quit school in the sixth grade so they could go to work, support the family, and help put food on the table. In search of a better life, Papa and Granny Lee moved to Florida and settled in an area known as Plant City. It didn't take long for them to start looking for a church, confident they had found the right one for their family when they found Southside Pentecostal Church of God, pastored by Sister Edna Mae Royster.

She was one of the most godly women I have ever known. Everything about her seemed to be custom-designed by God and untainted by the world. She was of average height and slightly overweight, with red hair that was always freshly fixed in large curls pinned up on the top of her head. The only thing she wore on her face was a pair of oversized glasses that sat on the apples of her cheeks when she smiled. Her eyes were soft-brown, and when she looked at you, you could feel genuine love radiating from them.

Before each service, you could hear her in her office praying for God to use her as He saw fit and to not let one person leave church that day lost. Prior to coming into the sanctuary, she would put on a minister's robe over her dress as another layer of modesty and respect for the position that God had placed her in. Then, she would walk up and down each aisle, greeting every one of the sheep God had entrusted to her. She would then take up her seat on the side of the choir while the associate pastor opened the service with prayer and prayer requests.

I'll never forget the story Pastor Royster told us about being called by God to start a church. In those days, it was almost unheard of for a woman to preach, much less pastor in the Pentecostal Church of God Association. The organization was staunch in its belief in the scripture that says women are to keep silent in the church. Pastor Royster would tell of having a dream in which she was standing over an open pit and could see into hell. There were hundreds of people screaming in torment, with flames of fire licking at their bodies. They were looking up and reaching for help. As she recalled, there were other people in the dream standing around the pit with her, most of whom were men. On the ground beside the pit were ropes, and she heard a voice she knew to be God say, "Throw them a rope." She ignored the voice, knowing that it must be talking to one of the others standing with her. Again, she heard, "Throw them a rope."

This time she said, "Lord, surely you don't mean me?! There are men here. Let one of them throw the rope."

That is when she heard God say, "Does it matter who throws the rope as long as the soul is saved?" She woke from the dream with the realization that God was calling her to start the Southside Pentecostal Church of God, and she did. Over the years, she was instrumental in leading countless souls to salvation, and it all started with obedience to the voice of God that came to her in a dream.

I have no doubt it is because of her obedience that so many of my own family, including myself, were saved. Had I not attended Sunday school and learned about Jesus or watched as Pastor Royster led so many in the sinners' prayer, I may not have known how to give my life to Jesus that night in my room when He tugged on my heart.

I never realized until now, in writing this book, just how much of my life was impacted by her obedience for it was in this church and with the people of its congregation that I would experience so much of my life. This is where I attended Sunday school, discovered my passion for singing, got baptized with the Holy Ghost, spoke in tongues, found my life-long best friend, fell in love for the first time, and saw countless people get saved. This church is where my grandparents' funerals were held, where I got married to the wrong man, and where I cried uncontrollably when they closed the doors for the last time.

It was my upbringing in this church that first exposed me to demonic possession and deliverance at a very young age. Pastor Royster had many gifts; not least among them were discernment and deliverance. Whenever someone new came to church, they were welcomed with open arms; however, as the shepherd of our flock, she was always on the lookout for anything or anyone who might bring us harm. If she discerned there was a threat, she would confront it head on, yet always allowing for restoration and reformation.

I remember one deliverance specifically. A new couple started coming to church. He was a larger man, who stood over six feet and weighed around three hundred pounds. He had sandy blond hair and sideburns. His hair was fine yet thick, and he had a habit of swinging his head to keep it out of his eyes. The man wore glasses with silver metal frames that were square-shaped and framed his hazel eyes. His shirts always seemed to be on the cusp of bursting open to reveal what was barely hidden in the first place. There was never a time when you couldn't see his stomach through the holes made by buttons that were overworked and underpaid. He often wore bell-bottomed, polyester dress pants with his shirt tucked inside. Completing the ensemble were a brown leather belt, well-worn cowboy boots, and a black Bible whose pages had shiny, red edges.

His wife was the complete opposite. She seemed short compared to him, and her lack of height was exaggerated by the slight bend in her back that caused her to walk hunched over. Her build was very small, and I found myself thinking that if she were to turn sideways, she may even disappear. She had thin light-brown hair that was straight and so long she sat on it each time she would sit down. She too had glasses, but hers were round and tinted, never revealing the true color of her eyes. The peasant tops and dresses she wore made it obvious that comfort was more important to her than fashion though everything she wore swallowed her slight frame.

The couple had been coming to church for a few weeks when deliverance came for the small, frail woman. After singing several songs from the Red Church Hymnal, a Pentecostal staple, Pastor Royster asked if anyone wanted prayer. A few members of the congregation went to the front of the church, wanting prayer for various reasons. Some wanted prayer to recover from illness. Some wanted God's favor in finding a new job. Others simply wanted to feel closer to Him.

At the end of the prayer line stood the couple. She was crying inconsolably. He placed his arm around her in support, rubbing her back, seeming to simply reassure her of his presence. They reached the place where Pastor Royster stood. She asked the woman if she was ready to surrender to the drawing of the Holy Ghost. When the woman nodded in agreement, Pastor Royster raised her hand and motioned for the church elders to come aid her in praying for the woman.

She turned to the associate pastor and gave instruction to start the precautions he and the other elders were taught to implement whenever a demonic deliverance was going to take place. The precautions started with two or more elders gathering all of us children together at the back of the church, drawing a cross on our foreheads with anointed extra virgin olive oil, praying, "God would shelter and protect us from any demon that may try to enter us," and instructing us to repeat the mantra, "I plead the blood of Jesus. I plead the blood of Jesus." Once this step was completed, one elder would stay with us children while the others rushed to the side of Pastor Royster with their Bibles in hand.

While the elders were anointing us children, Pastor Royster was keeping the woman's attention by holding her hand, reassuring her of God's love and asking her to acknowledge she wanted to be delivered.

The woman cried out, saying, "I don't want to live this way anymore. I want to live for God. I want to be free!"

Once she was confident we children were safe and the woman truly wanted deliverance, I watched as the sweet, gentle demeanor of my pastor turned to a commanding, authoritative language I did not understand. She grabbed the woman's face with her hands in a way that was both forceful and gentle, looking directly into the woman's eyes. She spoke to the demon and demanded that it reveal its name. This command must have angered the malevolent spirit because the woman's soft meek voice was replaced by a deep, eerie growl that sounded more animalistic than human when it spoke inaudibly. Pastor Royster was not deterred. She continued to speak in tongues, which further angered the evil spirit, causing it to throw four grown, large men across the room and onto the floor, including the woman's husband. Pastor Royster reached one of her hands out for her Bible.

A nearby elder placed the Bible in her hands, already opened to Mark chapter 5, which tells the story of Jesus delivering a man possessed by a host of demons called legion. Pastor Royster continued to pray in tongues while she put the Bible on the woman's abdomen and asked once again for the demon to reveal its name. As soon as the Bible touched the woman, she calmed down, growled something, and vomited into the trash container being held in front of her. She collapsed on the floor under the power of the Holy Ghost. Everyone who had been praying for her deliverance now turned their attention to chasing the unseen evil out of the church doors and off the property.

Confident that the deliverance was complete, someone started playing a song of victory on the piano that was accompanied by an outbreak of the Holy Ghost with dancing, shouting, and speaking in tongues. The service ended when the woman woke from being "slain in the Spirit" and gave testimony of the miracle God performed for her that night.

Chapter 9

Finally, my brethren, be strong in the Lord,
and in the power of His might. Put on the
whole armor of God, that ye may be able
to stand against the wiles of the devil. For
we wrestle not against flesh and blood, but
against principalities, against powers, against
the rulers of the darkness of this world,
against spiritual wickedness in high places.

—Ephesians 6:10–12

I am aware that my experiences seem far-fetched and unbelievable unless you yourself have experiences like mine or you are of the same or similar faith. I am sharing my experiences because it is imperative that you understand, as you read my story, that I have never been sheltered from the reality that evil exists and we are in a constant battle with it regardless of age, race, religion, gender, belief, or relation. With that in mind, please understand my mother was attempting to prepare me for battle on the way home from the airport that day. She felt she was equipping me with the knowledge of what we were truly fighting. The enemy was not my father, but an evil; with such a stronghold on him, it would eventually take him to his grave.

Mama started by telling me that she loved me and Daddy loved me too. I watched as she gathered her composure and prayed for God to help me understand what she was about to tell me. This incident took place shortly after I was born.

Having been raised in church, knowing right from wrong, Mama knew she had fallen away from God. Throughout her pregnancy with me, she felt a calling to repent and rededicate her life to God. However, each time she saw the evidence of me in the mirror or felt me kick, guilt and shame for being unwed and pregnant would hold her back from the surrender she so desperately wanted. After I was born, my Nana and Papa invited her to come to a tent revival they were having and bring me with her. My father was out of town on a "business" trip, so Mama decided to accept the invitation.

When she arrived, she was surprised to see that the tent was already filled with people there to hear Papa preach a fiery word from God. The service had not yet started when Nana spotted Mama making her way to a vacant seat in the back with me in tow. Nana wound her way through the crowd to where Mama sat. She urged her to move to the front row, off to the side where the organ was located. This way, Nana could help care for me once she was finished playing the music. Mama was grateful for her kindness, though she was sure Nana also wanted to show me off and play with me while Papa was preaching. Sure enough, as soon as the music was over and Papa took to the podium, Nana eased me out of Mama's arms and sat beside her.

She couldn't remember what songs were sung. She couldn't remember what either Papa or Nana was wearing. She didn't remember what the scripture was that Papa preached from. There were lots of things she would never remember, but what she could never forget was that this night changed her life forever. This was the night she rededicated her life to God, and He rewarded her by filling her with His Holy Ghost.

Papa gave an altar call, bidding anyone and everyone to come. If you were lost, hurting, sick, or lonely, whatever your need, come. She did! Papa asked her if she was ready to stop running, to give up, to surrender. The moment she said yes! Papa laid his hand on her forehead ever so gently, and she immediately hit the floor, slain in the Spirit! She didn't remember how long she was out, only that when she woke up she tried to talk, but the words coming out were not English. They were in an unknown language and accompanied by a sensation she felt all over her body like she had never known before.

When she left the revival that night, Mama was excited for the future. She was a new creation, and she was determined to never again turn away from God.

It had been a few days since Mama's personal encounter with God. She was still overwhelmed by the love she felt that night and every night since. That may have been the reason behind her excitement when Daddy returned from his business trip and introduced her to his new friend Don. Don was an evangelist with a tent ministry just like Papa. She couldn't remember where Daddy met Don, but they had become fast friends, spending all of their time together. After some discussion and quite a bit of "prayer," the two decided they would set the tent up in Tampa and launch a "Whirlwind Revival."

At Daddy's insistence, Mama attended the nightly services. Sure, Don could preach, but something inside Mama cautioned her that things were not as they seemed, to be watchful and not get caught up in the theatrics of his ministry. So with her newly found gift of discernment, each night, Mama sat beside Don's wife and watched the service. Don and Daddy had become so close that Daddy was now opening the service every night with a welcome to the people, a prayer for God's blessing, and an exuberant introduction of Don, the man responsible for bringing God to the tent each night. Once he was introduced, Don would pump up the crowd with hoops, hollers, and promises of Holy Ghost movements. Once the crowd was salivating with hunger for the tease to be fulfilled, he would motion for the organist to start her role in this lively drama to which the pleasantly plump and scantily dressed woman would launch into playing with as much gusto as she could conjure while bouncing and shaking her well-endowed bosom. Before long, someone in the congregation would let out a squeal and start dancing all over the tent. Apparently, it was contagious. By the time the first song was finished, half of the people had joined in the dancing and shouting, including my daddy. Mama couldn't help but notice the look of embarrassment on the face of Don's wife, as if she were guilty by association of the blasphemy that was taking place.

All of a sudden, the reason for the debacle became clear to Mama as she watched Daddy and Don each grab a wicker basket in unison. They started dancing down opposite aisles with the basket extended so those in attendance could show their love for God with a generous donation to the ministry. Mama knew this wasn't right. This wasn't the will of God. These people were homeless, hungry, and hurting in most cases, yet they were being robbed of what little they had in the name of God. Knowing there was nothing she could do to stop this fleecing from happening, Mama whispered to Don's wife her plans to go to our rented hotel suite so she could feed me, and she slipped out of the tent with me in her arms.

The hotel was old and dingy, certainly not in the best part of town, but Mama was grateful for the refuge it provided from the charade taking place across the street. She finished feeding me, rocked me to sleep, and laid me on a blanket on the floor by her side of the bed. Sure that I was down for the night, she grabbed her Bible from the bedside table and made her way to the main room of the suite. She wanted to remind herself of the true nature of God, to feel His embrace as she had that night at Papa's revival. As she sat there reading, the embrace started to manifest. It felt as though warm honey had saturated every part of her being, physical, mental, emotional, and spiritual. In that moment, she knew what she had was the real thing. There was nothing nor anyone who could take away the love she felt from her Father or for Him.

She did not have any idea just how much she was going to need this confidence in her faith, but she was about to.

The service had been over for hours. Worried that something terrible may have happened to Daddy, Mama waited up. She should not have.

It was after midnight when the three of them walked in. It was Daddy, Don, and a woman whom Mama recognized as the provocative and plump organ player. This woman certainly wasn't Don's sweet wife, whom Mama knew. Mama somehow sensed Don's wife must be just as scared and helpless as she was feeling right about now. This woman did not seem helpless or afraid. She was laughing, hanging all over Don, and letting him grope her without any "no trespassing" signs.

Mama was shocked and disgusted by this man who portrayed himself to be a servant and minister for God, yet his true nature revealed itself as cruel, irreverent, and evil, taking advantage of those most vulnerable for profit and having no loyalty to his marriage covenant.

The reason for their late arrival was evident by the reek of whiskey on all of them. Mama knew just how dangerous an intoxicated Skip could be, so in an effort to avoid confrontation, she simply closed her Bible and started toward the bedroom. Daddy caught her arm as she passed by him. "Have a drink with us, baby." Not much of a drinker before or after her encounter with salvation, Mama declined. Daddy insisted, yet Mama refused once again. Her refusal was an embarrassment. She disobeyed his order in front of his new friends.

He rewarded her by punching her in the face and knocking her to the floor. There would be no intervention from Don or "Plump Patty." Daddy excused himself so he could "teach his wife a lesson." He proceeded to drag her to the bedroom by her hair. Once there, he commenced with her punishment, delivering blow after blow until he could no longer stand due to exhaustion and whiskey. Finally, he undressed and passed out on the bed.

With me still asleep on the pallet she made, Mama tried to muffle her cries as she crawled over me and eased onto her side of the bed. She reached for her Bible. It landed in the center of the bed sometime during her beating. She started to read, taking turns reading, then praying both in silence for fear she might wake him. My mother didn't understand why this was her lot in life. She didn't understand why this man couldn't be the charming, charismatic man that she loved all of the time. Mostly, she didn't understand how she could not have seen this side of him before she tied her life to him forever by having his child.

His child? No, that isn't right. This is her child. I was her child.

I was her child! As she sat there making that silent declaration in her spirit, he sat up instantly, eyes wide and head turned toward her. He seemed even bigger than he actually was. Before passing out, he had undressed, and she could see the veins in his body bulging as if they were going to burst at any moment. His heart was beating so hard and fast it was visible to her naked eye. She was terrified. After all, she had just suffered a beating at this man's hands that left her bloody, bruised, broken, and battered. She stared at him as he started to speak. The voices coming from him were not his.

She recalled a child's voice, a woman's voice, and a malevolent voice as he asked her, "Who am I?"

With all of the strength she could muster, she replied, "You are Skip."

Again and again, he asked, "Who am I?"

And each time, she would reply, "You are Skip."

Suddenly, all of the voices faded with the exception of the malevolent one. Daddy turned to look at Mama, but it wasn't Daddy that she saw in his eyes when he demanded, "I said, WHO AM I?"

She knew exactly who it was when she answered, "You are Satan!"

He replied, "That's right! I have got him, and I will soon have you."

My mama defied him. She may have been scared in the natural, but her spirit felt as though she was standing on the shoulders of a giant, facing down a bully who doesn't realize just how small he is. With the backbone of Samson, she stared directly into his eyes and told that demon, "You will NEVER have me. I belong to God."

The demon replied, "You don't believe me? Watch this. I can make him do anything I want him to." At this, my father got up from the bed and walked around to my mother's bedside, where I lay sleeping on the floor. He picked his foot up and put it on my head and said to my mama, "I can make him do anything I want him to. I can make him crush her head with his foot if I so desire." That is when my beautiful, beaten, skinny little mama realized the authority given by God when she rededicated her life to Him.

She told the demon she and I were covered by the blood of Jesus and, "Satan, you can't cross the bloodline!"

Immediately, he removed his foot from my head and walked back to his side of the bed and lay down without another word. Mama said that when he woke up the next morning, he did not remember any of what had happened, but she did.

Chapter 10

I guess I have known pretty much my entire life that I have what they call an "old soul." I never really thought about it much until now, but looking back, I can see how I was always older than my years. I was drawn into adult conversations. I enjoyed being with adults more so than kids my own age, save a very few. I knew how to blend into the surroundings so the grown-ups wouldn't notice me while they were interacting. This allowed me to pick up and process information that I probably should not have been privy to as a child. Being more mature than my age is most likely why I remember things so vividly when most people have a hard time remembering fine details of memories at such a young age.

I can promise you, for as long as I live, I will remember that car ride home. I won't remember it for the airplanes taking off so close to me that I could feel the rumble of their engines or the fact that I could almost reach out and touch them. I won't remember it for the blue sky with its cotton clouds that were made up of familiar shapes when I squinted my eyes just right. I won't remember it for the sound of the radio blaring those southern gospel quartets singing songs that made my skin turn into shriveled up goose bumps. No, I will forever remember that day as the beginning of a bond being built with my mama that would last a lifetime. I will remember every syllable of every word she spoke when telling me her story. It was crucial that I remember every detail. This was the day that she entrusted me with the knowledge of what she, and now we, were fighting and she began to teach me how to fight it. Mama asked me if I was ready to ask Jesus into my heart, and I shared with her how Jesus had beckoned me—how I asked Him to live in my heart, kneeling beside my bed while saying my prayers. Mama told me it was important that I pray every day, try to read the Bible so I could learn more about Jesus, put on the armor of God as soon as my feet touch the floor each morning, and ask Him to fill me with His Holy Ghost.

Mama said these were the basics. She would guide me and teach me other things along the way, as would other warrior women such as Granny, Pastor Royster, and Aunt Teeney. She said God would send many people throughout my life to help me mature into the person He wants me to be, but I should always make sure to use the gift of discernment that would come with the baptism of the Holy Ghost. Until I received my baptism, Mama and these three women would be watching over me along with God, of course!

We arrived home from the airport just before dusk. I remember opening the door to get out of the car with a sense of sadness for the loss of my childhood. I knew the little girl in me had to take a backseat to the older, wiser version of myself. I had to be mindful in all circumstances at all times. I could no longer allow the child I once was to freely exist in my life. I must always be conscious of any danger, real or just perceived.

Chapter 11

I'm not exactly sure how long my father was gone, but to me, it seemed like a lifetime, and I LOVE IT! So many good things happened while he was gone, and I began to believe we were starting a new life without him. This new life began when we moved from that little white house, where I first saw the monster that lived inside Daddy.

Mama found a little one-bedroom apartment not too far from my grandparents. It was a small complex altogether, consisting of eight ground-floor apartments in two main buildings, reserved for residents over the age of fifty-five. These apartments held the secret of an in-ground pool nestled between them, hidden and protected for residents only.

On the outer edge of the property was a separate building that stood alone at the end of a lazy side street. That is where we lived. It reminded me of the buildings in Greece that I had seen pictured in magazines and on television with their stark white walls. I always imagined it was a result of being bleached by the salty sea water. There was no salty seawater that caused this effect on our building. It was simply old and weathered by time and neglect. It didn't bother me. I thought it was one of many characteristics that gave it a unique charm. Another was the multipaned windows that swung out when you opened them and allowed the curtains to billow in the breeze on a windy day.

The building was two-story with four apartments, two on the ground floor and two on the top. Each apartment had its own entrance. The ones on the top floor came complete with spiral staircases, perfect for pretending to be a princess stuck in a tower waiting for her Prince Charming to defeat the dragon and rescue her.

The property surrounding the building wasn't too big or too small. It had parking spaces marked for each apartment on their respective sides and extra space in the front should it be needed for company.

It was guarded by a small wooden fence that looked like it belonged more on a ranch to corral horses than in front of our complex. The make-shift fence separated the extra parking spaces from the apartment, leaving an area in front of the building for the resident kids to play and enjoy being kids.

The apartment itself was old and a little shabby, but Mama cleaned it and put her own personal touch in the decorating, which made it feel like home.

Our apartment was on the bottom left if you were standing outside, facing the building. The two apartments on the second floor were vacant when we first moved in; however, the other bottom apartment to our right was occupied by some of the landlord's family that included two of his grandsons, Sambo and Jimbo. At least, that is what their parents and grandparents called them, which I have no doubt were their nicknames. It didn't take long for us to become friends or for me to develop my first and second crush!

Back then, it seemed my mama's best friend, Sue, and her children, Missy, Nikki, and Jason, were always at our home. I LOVED having them around. They have always been more like family than friends. They were also a welcome and much-needed distraction from the trauma I had experienced. Being with them allowed me to be a kid again. We played outside until well after dark, riding our bikes, playing in mud puddles, playing hide and seek, swimming in the pool, and just doing the things kids do.

I was so very grateful to each one of them.

Jason was the youngest, super cute with his blue eyes, curly blond hair, and dimples. Those dimples! There was no chance any of the Parker kids would escape having them as both their mama and daddy had them. Their dimples were so deep that you could poke your finger inside if you dared.

Jason was always pestering and pulling pranks on us girls. As annoying as he could be, there were valuable lessons he taught us like building a fort with pillows, blankets, and kitchen chairs. Nobody was better at constructing things than Jason! Tired of being the only boy and the guinea pig for our girly experiments, I am pretty sure it was him who made first contact with Sambo and Jimbo, starting a friendship over the simple fact that they were boys who wanted to play with other boys.

Next there was Missy. She was our protector and the closest thing I have ever had to a big sister. She was also the oldest and most athletic. She is what I think of when I imagine the standard for American beauty. She has naturally beautiful blond hair, blue eyes, a slender hour-glass figure, and those Parker dimples.

Missy was a track star throughout her years in school, and I remember being in awe of how fast she could run and wishing I could run like her, so fast it must have felt like flying. Missy never let us out of her sight, and she never let anyone bully or hurt us either. She was a rock for me, and I am not sure that I ever told her how much that meant to me, then or now.

Then there was Nikki. She was closest to my age at just shy of a year older and shared my first name, Angela, though we called her Nikki after her middle name, Nicole. To this day, I don't think I have ever seen someone more naturally beautiful. She has hair that is almost black, eyes that are a golden color somewhere between brown and green, and those dimples I envy to this day. I always dreamed of waking up one day and looking in the mirror to see that I had been transformed into someone with her beauty.

As pretty as she was, Nikki never made me feel anything less than her equal. Throughout my adolescence, I was an introvert. Not Nikki! She was as much an extrovert as I was an introvert. Friends came easily for her, but she never left me behind. If they wanted to hang around with Nikki, then they had to include me as well.

The one issue I had? The boys always liked Nikki, ALWAYS! This was a constant that I would come to know and expect throughout our lives together. It was always the same, whether we were at school, cheerleading, or just hanging around the neighborhood; however, it all started here with Sambo and Jimbo.

I can't blame Nikki for my unrequited love as I am positive I never expressed it most likely due to a paralyzing shyness when the boys were around. Not willing to risk rejection, I simply forgot about my crush and focused on what really mattered at eight, riding my bike with no hands!

So I played, and I laughed, and I had the time of my life just being a kid.

I was finally loving my life as a carefree little girl should, but what I loved most was bedtime.

Each night, Mama would put Tracy and me in bed with her, tell us stories from the Bible, and teach us about Jesus. She encouraged us to ask questions, and she made sure that we knew how to pray and put on the "whole armor of God."

Mama would say, "Girls, always remember that we are soldiers in the Army of God. As soldiers, we must always have our armor on.

"We start with the BELT of TRUTH! Make sure to always tell the truth, seek the truth, and walk in truth! It is the truth that sets us free!

"Secondly, we put on the BREASTPLATE of RIGHTEOUSNESS! This righteousness is not ours. It belongs to Jesus. He has given it to us so no one can say we are unworthy or undeserving of Christ's love and forgiveness.

"Next come the SHOES of READINESS and PEACE! These shoes give us the power to have peace in all circumstances and situations. No matter how much fear or anxiety the enemy tries to cause, he has no power because we walk in the peace of God.

"Our shoes are followed by our SHIELD of FAITH! Always remember Jesus is in control of everything, and He will take care of you because of His love for you. No matter what the circumstances may look like, never let the circumstances you see cause you to waiver in your assurance that God will work all things out in your favor!

"The last piece of armor we put on is the HELMET of SALVATION! Because we have all asked Jesus into our hearts, we are saved. Never let anyone tell you differently. Jesus died to give us the gift of salvation. No one can take that gift from you. Only you can lay it down. Never do that! If you do, just remember, Jesus will always be there with open arms to welcome you back because He loves you.

"Once we have finished putting our armor on, it is time we take up our weapons! The SWORD of the SPIRIT, which is the WORD of GOD!

"Finally, we engage our secret weapon, PRAYER! We pray in all situations for all situations! God will always hear the prayers of His children and answer them. It won't always be the answer we want to hear, but He will always answer in His timing."

By the time she was finished, Tracy was usually asleep, but not me. I was wide awake, hanging on every word she was saying and finding myself falling more and more in love with both Mama and Jesus. I could feel that Jesus loved me and wanted me. Somehow I knew He wanted me to know what pure, unconditional, everlasting love felt like.

This became our routine every night, and I am eternally grateful to my mama for it. The foundation she helped build in me at such a young age has stood the test of time and remains still. I have been through many, many storms that most believe should have taken me under and destroyed me, but they don't know how solid my foundation is!

With that said, my foundation was about to be put to its first test. I had naively allowed myself to be lulled into a false sense of happiness and security, but a storm was coming and the facade of safety would soon be shattered, though my foundation would not waiver.

Chapter 12

One day, the phone rang. I watched as Mama turned white as a ghost the moment she heard the voice on the other end of the line. She hung up and told me to help get my sister in the car. We were going to the airport to pick my father up. WHAT?! This could not be happening! Surely, he wasn't coming back now! He had been gone for so long—at least a couple of years or more. I was now eight, maybe nine, and my sister was four or five. She wouldn't even know him, and I didn't want to know him. Life had been so good without him.

During the entire car ride to the airport, my mama didn't say a word. She only made the occasional "Shhhh!" to Tracy in a futile effort to soothe her cries. Perhaps Tracy could sense the fear Mama was feeling the same way I could. It was going to be a bad night. I could feel it in every ounce of me. Looking back at my younger self, I have no doubt that it was the gift of discernment working in my life even then. I knew the exchange between my parents on the phone, or rather the lack of exchange, meant that he was angry about something. What reason could he possibly have for being angry with Mama? He had been gone for so long, and there was no way she could have done anything. Besides, he surely missed her, didn't he?

The closer we got to the airport, the more nauseous I became. The darkness seemed thicker, heavier than usual. It was as if the very air outside was trying to get in and suffocate us with the fear of what might come. When we arrived, I saw my father standing at the curb waiting for us. My stomach leaped in an attempt to hide behind my backbone. The memories of everything I had seen him do came flooding back. I was so scared. He turned to face us, and my fears were realized when I saw his eyes.

I recognized that look of rage—that same look I had seen twice before, once when I found him choking Mama with a belt while she was bound, naked to a chair, and again when he beat a man simply because he "thought" the man was looking at my mother. I prayed so hard that I would never see it again, yet here it was—that look that didn't care about anyone, that look that wanted to hurt, wanted to destroy, and wanted to kill!

At the sight of him, I watched Mama change from the strong, funny, confident, and beautiful woman she had been all the time he was gone into a scared, weak, and desperate person, terrified of what was sure to come now that this man had returned to invade our happy, peaceful world.

As we pulled up beside him, Mama stopped the car, got out, and hurried around to climb into the passenger's side and shut the door. Always one to make sure he kept up appearances in public, my father put a smile on his face as he greeted us all with a fake and syrupy "There's my girls!" He then walked to the back of the car, opened the trunk, and ever-so-gently placed his luggage inside before closing the lid. He climbed into the driver's seat and looked over his shoulder at Tracy and me before starting our long drive home.

As we were leaving the airport, I tried to focus on the huge airplanes that were taking off. The ones landing never grabbed my attention because all I wanted to do was escape, so I trained my focus on the ones making their ascent into the vast blue unknown. I wanted to go anywhere that he wasn't. As I watched one taxi onto the runway, I tried to imagine where it was headed. What did the inside of the plane look like? What were the people like who were on board the flight? Were they going away forever or just for a visit?

I was brought back to reality by the sound of my father's fist punching my mother in the face and my sister screaming from the terror she must be feeling witnessing this. He had to assert his dominance, and abuse was his weapon of choice. My mama cowered in the seat, crying, cradling her face in her hands as she pressed herself firmly against the door in a fruitless effort to escape his reach. He unleashed a barrage of open-handed hits on her tiny body anywhere he could—head, arms, and legs. It didn't matter; he just wanted to hurt her.

Daddy started yelling at Mama that it was her own fault. She shouldn't be prying into his business. She shouldn't be asking questions that she doesn't want to know the answers to. Her job was to be a mother to his daughters and a loving, doting wife to him. It was not her business to call his friends or professional acquaintances and ask where he was or what he was doing.

Gathering the tidbits of what I could from this one-sided conversation, it seemed that when my father left town, he gave my mother what he thought was plenty of money to live on while he was gone. She was meant to move, pay the bills, feed us, and clothe us with whatever measly amount he gave her. Of course, it didn't last nearly as long as his "business" trip did. We had been relying on Mama's meager wages and her parents, Granny and Papa. They were the only reason we even had food to eat.

Granny and Papa were amazing! They were my favorite people in the entire world, but they were definitely people of humble means. I can remember Granny sewing clothes out of old flour sacks she saved once they were empty and Papa always wearing overalls because they were good enough for working in the yard, working on the car, going fishing, or going to church. Just change the undershirt that you wore with them, and you were good to go. Granny and Papa did everything they could to help us, but they just didn't have anything left to help with. Tired of living on flour, gravy, and hoe bread, my mama started making calls, trying to find Daddy in hopes that he would send money so she could feed us and keep a roof over our heads.

After weeks of searching and dozens of unreturned calls, she was finally given an international number for a residence in Costa Rica. When she called, a woman answered. Mama asked for "Skip." The woman responded naturally, "Who's calling?" to which Mama replied, "This is his wife, Judy."

The woman on the other end said, "Excuse me, but that is not possible! This is his wife, Abbie." Mama hung up the phone in shock! His wife?!

Apparently, his double life had been exposed in that call, and he was here to punish Mama for destroying the perfectly good setup he had going.

I don't think I will ever forget the sight of Mama pressed up against that car door with her knees jammed in her chest, her head tucked down into them, and her entire body shaking. Whether it was from fear, pain, or just pure shock, to this day I can't say, but what I can say is that it seemed my father had found no further need to hide his demons.

When we arrived home that evening, without saying a word, Mama started dinner while Daddy took a shower and made some phone calls. I thought the worst was behind us for the night as I watched television with Tracy curled up beside me on the couch, finally asleep. Little did I know that he was just getting started.

When he came out of the bedroom, his plate was waiting on the coffee table in front of the couch along with a glass of sweet iced tea.

For dinner, Mama had made spaghetti with meat sauce, salad, and garlic bread. It was one of my favorites. I was just about to ease Tracy off my leg and go to the small, two-chair table in the kitchen when it seemed all hell broke loose. Without a word of warning, Daddy picked up his plate and threw it against the wall, just barely missing Mama's head. It was followed by a mason jar of iced tea. Both now lay shattered on the floor. He continued his rampage by emptying the pot containing the rest of what was to be our dinner and then spreading it with his feet, making sure to grind it into the freshly mopped surface my mother had scrubbed just the day before.

The show wasn't over. He burst into a litany of name-calling and accusations, all of them ending with why this was all her fault. She needed to learn her lesson, and if this was how she had to learn, then so be it! He grabbed her by her hair, pushed her to the floor, and dragged her until she was sitting in the middle of the mess he'd made with our dinner. He growled through clenched teeth. "Look what you made me do. Clean it up, now!" He then turned to me and said, "Angela, go make me something to eat."

What? Me? I didn't know how to cook! Sure, I watched Mama cook. I even helped her several times, but I had no idea how to cook a meal myself. I was terrified that I would mess up and he would do to me what he'd done to Mama. I started to cry, but I was careful not to let him see or hear me for fear of his temper. Thankfully, Daddy was now seated on the couch, watching television as if nothing had happened, waiting for his meal.

I was standing at the stove, frozen, when I felt Mama tug at my shorts. I looked down at her with what I am sure she recognized as a look of fear and panic. She motioned for me to lean down, and when I did, she whispered in my ear for me to get the two boxes of macaroni and cheese out of the cabinet along with the two cans of tuna beside them. She would tell me what to do step by step. She surprised me when, while whispering in my ear, she asked, with a bruised and beaten face, if I'd remembered to put my armor on that morning. I forced a smile in response to hers, and I nodded.

She whispered, "Good, then no weapon formed against us can prosper! Not even this one."

By this time, Tracy was awake. She came into the kitchen and sat down at Mama's side on the floor. I watched as Mama cleaned up the evidence of my father's outburst, though she could not clean up the evidence he left on her face. I prayed I would never see my mother this way again, yet here she was with her face swollen and bruised and her eyes barely able to open. My heart was broken. I knew that Jesus loved Mama the same way He loved me, but I did not understand why He would allow Daddy to hurt her the way he did. I pulled a dishcloth from the drawer beside the stove and wrapped it around some ice cubes I'd collected from the tray in the freezer. I placed the ice-packed dishcloth on Mama's face as gently as I could. She grabbed my hand and squeezed it in a silent show of appreciation. As I smiled down at her, I hoped she would know how sorry I was that she had suffered so much abuse at the hands of my father.

There was nothing more that either of us could say or do to change the circumstances we now found ourselves in, so one by one, Mama gave me the instructions I needed to make macaroni and cheese with tuna fish. I followed them exactly.

When I was finished, I filled a plate with the fruits of my labor and poured Daddy a new glass of iced tea. I carried them both to him and was rewarded with a smile as he said, "Thank you, baby."

Daddy acted as if all was right with the world and he'd done nothing wrong, but he had, and the effects of his actions created a ripple effect in several areas of my life, some good and some not so good. First, him forcing me to cook awakened a passion and talent within me that would last a lifetime. Secondly, I learned my father had another wife, possibly another family, which was the beginning of opening my eyes to the reality that there was nothing he would not do, no line he would not cross. Next, it strengthened the bond I had with my mother. We learned to cling to one another because we were the only ones who knew what we were going through. Sure, Tracy was there, but she was still too young to comprehend what was happening, thank God. Speaking of God, this is where I started to question why He would allow us to suffer so much. I loved Him, and I knew He loved me, but why didn't He stop this from happening? After all, He is God, and He can do anything.

I never realized until right now, while writing this memory, that this is where my internal tug-of-war began. The start of a struggle was justifying in my mind how a loving, caring, all-knowing, all-power-ful God would not intervene on behalf of those who love Him and serve Him when He absolutely has the ability to.

I am not quite ready to give you my answer to this question, but it will come. Stick with me a while longer.

Chapter 13

For the next week or so, things were as normal as they could be when you live with someone who can go from the funniest, kindest, most loving man you know to the monster that haunts your dreams in an instant.

Yet again, a storm started brewing when our new, upstairs neighbors arrived.

I remember watching them carry their belongings up the stairs, the young newly married couple that would be our neighbors. They didn't seem to have much furniture as I only recall the sofa and its worn floral print cushions that were set against a shiny, stained, and varnished wooden frame. Most everything else they hauled up those stairs was shielded from my view by the garbage bag or box that held it.

She was short, slender, and pretty with her shoulder-length, thick, and curly brown hair. The first time I saw her, she was wearing a plaid button-up western shirt that was tied just above the waist of her cut-off jean shorts. Her ensemble was completed by white sneakers that were a contrast to her tanned legs.

He was slender as well and quite a bit taller than her, which allowed her head to fit just perfectly in the nook of his arm when they embraced. It was as if they were made for each other in the same way two connecting puzzle pieces were. He was more than a little handsome, with thick black hair and a smile that made him seem friendly and kind. Like her, he too was dressed for the task of moving that first day that I saw him, wearing a white T-shirt, black track shorts, and black canvas tennis shoes.

They appeared happy as they laughed and playfully teased one another in a way that I imagine is reserved for those in love. With every trip back to the truck they were unloading, I would see them pinch or grab one another and follow it up with a quick kiss. Their laughter was a welcome distraction from the yelling my father so often did. As I got lost in the beauty of the love displayed between them, I couldn't foresee that their arrival marked the beginning of a nightmare that would haunt my dreams for years to come.

It didn't take long for my father to befriend the man. Every evening, they would gather in either our living room, theirs, or at the bottom of the stairs and share stories. These stories were accompanied by beer and whiskey in large enough quantities to leave them both stumbling to their respective beds. This ritual was broken a few months after the couple moved in when my daddy decided he needed to introduce his new friend to some of his old friends. They drove off around ten in the morning, and by five that evening, the woman upstairs was knocking on our door. Mama opened the door, and the woman came rushing in. She was clearly upset. I could see that she'd been crying. She pleaded with Mama to help her find her husband. It wasn't like him to be gone all day and not call her. Something must have happened. Mama tried to calm the woman down by urging her to sit at the kitchen table while she poured her a glass of tea. As they sat there talking, I could hear the desperation in her voice as, once again, she begged Mama to help her find them. Mama listened, and then she told her that this was a common occurrence for my father. He often left for days at a time, and she was sure they were fine. The woman would not be deterred as this was not something her husband would ever do. Finally, my mother reluctantly agreed to take her to look for her husband. With that, the four of us—Mama, the woman, my sister and I—loaded up in our car and set out to find Daddy and his new drinking buddy. My mother knew exactly where to find them. As we approached the white house, I could see the terror starting to take up residence in her eyes. She stopped the car at the edge of the property next to a ditch. It was a large, old wooden farmhouse that seemed to be falling apart from neglect. In the yard, there were chickens and dogs running around freely. I could see a clothes line on the side of the house, and fastened to it were bedsheets of white, blue, and yellow. I remember thinking as they billowed in the breeze that their dance signaled that a storm was coming, and I was right.

From my vantage point, I could see that my father and the woman's husband were here. Daddy and our neighbor were on the front porch that ran the length of the house. They were surrounded by at least ten other people. All of them were laughing and drinking as if they didn't have a care in the world. Both men had half-dressed women perched on their laps with their faces buried in their breasts. At the sight of this, both my mother and the woman got out of the car and started to approach the house. That's when my father spotted them. He was ANGRY! Shoving the scantily dressed lady from his lap, Daddy threw his drink at my mother and hopped over the porch, grabbing a knife from the railing and now wielding it in his hand. My mama started running back toward the car as he gave chase, stumbling and screaming horrible names at her the whole time. He was just about to catch her when she jumped the ditch. He was either too drunk or too angry to jump the ditch himself, and he fell. This embarrassed him in front of his friends but gave her the time she needed to get back to the car, open the door, get in, and lock it.

The moment I heard the door lock engage, I looked up to see him standing at the window demanding through clenched teeth that Mama open the door. She didn't respond. She just put the car in gear and drove away, leaving the woman, her husband, and my father to work the matter out for themselves. On the way home, my mama didn't cry; she simply looked in the rearview mirror and said, "I am so sorry, girls. I am so sorry. I promise you that this will never happen again." With that, we went home, and she packed my father's things into those familiar green suitcases that he so often used. She put them outside and locked the doors. She had finally had enough, and it was over for her, but not for him.

Chapter 14

The next morning, Daddy's suitcases were still waiting for him outside the door of our apartment. Whether it was from being too drunk or too embarrassed, it didn't matter to me what his reason was. I was thankful he hadn't come home last night.

Mama must have seen the suitcases too, and they undoubtedly sounded her internal alarms that it was time to get out of there before he came home. I watched as she hurriedly gathered a week's worth of clothes for each of us, some picture albums, and a few sentimental keepsakes. She stuffed it all into a garbage bag and walked outside to put it in the car. I followed her out the door, tugging Tracy along by her hand. With our meager necessities loaded, the three of us climbed into the front seat of the monstrosity and drove away.

Shortly after returning from Costa Rica, Daddy, in desperate need of money, traded his classic 1965 Ford Mustang for some cash and this hideous-looking vehicle we now found ourselves escaping in. It was a 1967 Chevrolet Suburban painted a putrid color of yellow. It was a far cry from the pristine condition the Mustang had been kept in as it had dents, scratches, and rust everywhere. I recall the smell that took my breath away the first time I opened the door. I blamed Tracy for having an accident in her pants only to learn the stench was coming from the car. Once again, Mama worked her magic, and before long, the smell was replaced by the clean scent of bleach and Pine-Sol.

My nose seemed to catch a whiff of that Pine-Sol as we set out on our next adventure to my grandparents' house. Somehow, that fresh smell seemed to usher in the feeling of a fresh start. Regardless of what the future held, as I looked at my sister and my mama, I knew I wasn't alone. We had each other, and we had Jesus. That would be enough, more than enough.

Mama started singing "When We All Get to Granny's." It was a play on the old gospel hymn "When We All Get to Heaven." Tracy laughed as Mama sang and made faces at us to assuage any unsettled nerves or fears we may have had. I just smiled back at her, not allowing myself to get carried away or distracted in the moment. I had a mission, and that was my priority. I had to watch over them, both of them.

I was the oldest between Tracy and myself, and for some reason, Daddy made it no secret that I was his favorite child. He would never harm me. Everything I knew about him said that there was nothing he held in high enough regard that he would not destroy it—save me. He loved me in his own twisted way, and he never even came close to putting his hands on me. He told me many times throughout my life that I was his favorite, the only child that he made plans to conceive, and my mother would be the only woman he would ever truly love. Whether this declaration of love was true or not doesn't matter. Daddy believed it, and that would allow me the advantage of a surprise attack if the need ever presented itself.

The rest of the way to Granny's and Papa's house, I planned it all out in my mind. If he ever came back and tried to hurt Mama or Tracy, I would sneak into the kitchen and get the biggest, sharpest knife we owned. It would be in the knife block on the counter closest to the living room and closest to the front door. Once I had the knife, there would be a clear path to the area between the living room and the door. I'd stab him in the leg just to get his attention. He would look down to see where the pain was coming from. He would certainly be shocked to see me wielding the knife that cut him. I could use that as a distraction to insert myself between Daddy and his chosen victim. Then I would use the knife to threaten more harm if he wouldn't leave immediately. Once he was out the door, I would lock both locks and hurry to the window to watch him drive away. Once I had no doubt he was really gone, I would urge Mama to take the three of us somewhere safe and call the police. Yup! That is the plan. I now had a solid plan, and just in time, we'd arrived at Granny's and Papa's house. Now that I had a fail-safe plan, it was okay for me to rest, but only for a minute or two and only on the couch by the main door, so I'd be able to see who was coming and going. I laid my head on Granny's lap, and in an instant, I was asleep.

Eight hours later, I awoke at my grandparent's house. This was the safest and most peaceful I'd felt since before Daddy returned from Costa Rica. There was no place I would rather have been than here with Papa and Granny.

Granny and Papa had eight children, twenty-five grandchildren, and countless great-grandchildren throughout their lives together, yet they never failed to make me feel as if I was the most loved and cherished of all. I have no doubt each of us were made to feel this way, special and unique. Even so, the love I felt from my grandparents is a gift I have cherished, both then and now.

The memories I have of my grandparents are the best memories of my childhood. Even as an adult, when I reflect on my life, it is with them that I felt most loved.

It seemed they were always doing something that made me feel special. I can't begin to recall the number of times I would be in class and the buzz of the intercom system would come on. The sound triggered every kid's hopes they were being called to the school office to go home early. Then the voice that held us captive with anticipation would finally say, "Mr. or Mrs. So-and-So, could you please send Angela Wilkins to the office to go home?" I knew it was Granny and Papa! They had come to grant me parole from the rest of my school sentence for the day. I'd gather my things and run—no, walk quickly to the office where they would be waiting to greet me with warm mischievous smiles because Mama didn't know they were picking me up early.

After signing my pardon, we would walk to their car, a new four-door, yellow Ford Fairmont with a tan leather interior. Papa always parked just in front of the school in the disabled parking spaces. No matter how slow or feeble they became, the epitome of what it meant to be a gentleman, Papa made sure to open the door for Granny before returning to the driver's side of the car where he would open the back door and insert both their canes. He would then take up his position in the front driver's seat and start the car. I always sat in the back behind Granny, ready to burst with the excitement I felt just to be with them.

They never failed to have something special planned for my time spent with them. The first stop was always somewhere we could eat. Though no one could cook as good as Granny, there are times when we all want someone else to do the work so we can simply enjoy ourselves with those we love. Granny was no exception. Nine times out of ten, we ended up at their favorite home-style, country fare restaurant, Snellgroves. It is a small, quaint place where you never fail to run into someone you know. It is a place where people not only pray over their meals but also stop everything to respect others when they do the same. No doubt, that is part of the charm that draws you in and keeps you coming back. Not to mention, the food is excellent, and that's most likely why it's still in operation today, after all these years.

Once we had a proper meal together, my grandparents would often take me to a little five-and-dime store to let me pick out something for them to buy me. Thinking back, it seems my selections changed as I grew older. I started with candy and graduated to toys and eventually to clothing. Papa and Granny never had very much to spend, but somehow, they always managed to make me feel like the most fortunate kid in the world.

Once I'd chosen my reward for simply winning the grandparent lottery, I didn't linger in the store because I knew what was coming next. Dairy Queen! We always finished our adventure by stopping for a chocolate-dipped cone. My excitement was always evident by the smile plastered on my face. It was a result of the challenge I knew lay before me. Could I lick the ice cream fast enough to keep it from melting? Would I taste the sweetness of victory, or would the ice cream declare my defeat with the sticky residue it would inevitably leave on my face, clothes, and hands? I must admit there were several times in the beginning when the ice cream got the best of me, but once I learned how to properly lick and rotate in perfect timing, the war was won.

Those times with my loving grandparents were precious and invaluable to me. They are most definitely two of the people who were instrumental in shaping me into the person I am today. They taught me so much through their actions toward others as well as toward each other, kindness, generosity, respect, faith, loyalty, commitment, and love, and above all love.

That same love was evident this morning as I stumbled around the corner and into the kitchen. Everything that happened to bring us here seemed like a dream until I saw my mother's face. I found her sitting with Granny and Papa. She was seated on the side of the table closest to the opening that led to the living room, where I was peeking around the corner. Granny sat directly in front of her.

She was the dictionary definition of what you picture when you think of a southern grandmother. She was short and "pleasantly plump." She had shoulder-length gray hair that clung closely to her head, with the kind of spring curls that look like you just twirled it around your finger and held it for a minute or two before letting go. Her dress was made from a store-bought pattern and fashioned out of old flour sacks. It was white with small red flowers on it that were attached to green leaves and stems. The sleeves were short and slightly puffed, and the hem fell just below her calves. Over her dress, she wore an apron, cinched at her waist and covered in flour from the endless chore of making buttermilk biscuits. In mere moments, there would be no evidence of her painstaking labor as the biscuits would be devoured the instant their smell drifted into the vicinity of anyone nearby, taking advantage of the perfect vessel for sopping up Papa's sugarcane syrup.

I could smell a fresh batch in the oven as I watched the scene before me. Mama's hands were stretched across the table, and Granny's met them in a protective embrace. It seemed as though she was trying to erase all of Mama's pain and shelter her from feeling anymore. She didn't say a word. She simply let Mama cry while she comforted her by just being there to hold her hand.

Papa sat beside Granny wearing his work-around-the-house overalls with a white T-shirt that had faded grease stains on it from one of the countless times he'd worked on someone's car. What was left of his hair was combed back and to the side with wisps jetting out from under the arms of his black horn-rimmed glasses. He wasn't much taller than Granny, and it was a wonder to me that his short stature allowed room for the fathoms of love he held for her. I smiled, watching him sit with his hands resting atop the wooden cane he often used to smack one of us grandkids for back talking. We would try to run by on our way to the kitchen as he sat in his chair, thinking he had forgotten our indiscretion. He hadn't! It was never too hard, just a reminder to mind your manners and respect your elders.

Papa sat with his fingers folded in a way that made the fact that he was missing a thumb less noticeable.

The look on his face saddened me. It was that of a father who was hurting for his daughter all the while thinking of ways that he could exact retribution for every mark he could see and those he couldn't see, but could hear in her voice. Even at my young age, I knew that if Papa or anyone tried to confront my father in an attempt to make him answer for his abuse, they would likely suffer the same fate or worse. This is a horror I would later discover he was more than capable of. Thankfully, my mama and Granny were able to persuade Papa that returning violence for violence was not the answer. This was something better left in the hands of God. With that, I watched as they leaned in to embrace one another and prayed. The beauty of their voices lifted in unison to the source of their hope, strength, and comfort made me catch my breath as tears streamed down my cheeks. Not wanting to disturb this sacred moment, I joined them in silence as I watched from the doorway, and somehow I knew that God was going to move on our behalf.

We stayed with my grandparents that night and several nights that followed, and with each passing night, I felt a little more safe than the night before.

Chapter 15

Three weeks passed without any sign of my father. Whether it was caused by cabin fever or the simple need to get back to a semblance of a normal and independent routine I can't say, but Mama decided it was time to venture back out into the world we'd left waiting. The time had come for us to return to the little apartment we'd left so abruptly. In all truthfulness, I had no desire to leave the safe haven of Granny's and Papa's, but I didn't want to add to the stress Mama must be feeling at not knowing what awaited us at home. With all of the courage I could muster, I painted a smile on my face as we loaded our things into the awful "Yellow Whale" and backed out of my grandparents' driveway.

Their eyes betrayed the worry in their hearts and in their minds as they waved goodbye to us. Granny and Papa tried to smile, but no amount of effort could force the smiles to reach their eyes and erase the fear that had been there ever since Mama told them we were leaving. I knew what that fear felt like. It started in the pit of your stomach and grew until it consumed all of your thoughts. It was a feeling as familiar to me as my name, but not on this day.

What I felt now was not fear, it was sadness, sadness that we would no longer be with Granny and Papa every day. In fact, ever since I'd started my personal relationship with Jesus, fear had been replaced with a peace I cannot sufficiently describe. Was Daddy still dangerous? Absolutely! However, I somehow knew with unwavering confidence that Jesus was changing things in our lives for the better. There was a shift in the atmosphere, and He was orchestrating it.

As we drew closer to the apartment, Mama kept reassuring us that everything was going to be okay, "Girls, it's going to be fine. We are going to be fine. You know what? I bet it is just gonna be us from now on."

Though I appreciated her attempts at comforting us, I didn't need to hear it from Mama because I already knew it was going to be fine. Sure enough, when we arrived at the apartment, there was no sign of Daddy. Mama let out a huge sigh of relief as she turned the engine off and allowed her head to rest on the steering wheel for a while before hustling us out of the car and into the apartment.

When she opened the door, we walked in to find all of my father's belongings absent from the apartment as though he had never lived there at all. There were no clothes, shoes, suitcases, and not even a toothbrush to indicate he ever existed in this space. The feeling was surreal. I loved my daddy, and I would miss him, but I was not willing to trade his presence for my mama's safety. Nor did I want Tracy to witness his outbursts of rage any more than I wanted to witness them myself.

With a sense of gratitude for answered prayers, I quickly helped Mama unload the car. Once our things were unpacked and put away, Tracy and I got our baths while Mama made sloppy joes for dinner. We watched TV while we ate, and then we snuggled up in bed together where Mama resumed her duties of teaching us about Jesus.

When I close my eyes and think back to that day, I can still feel her arms as she pulled Tracy and me a little closer and hugged us a little tighter than usual.

Later that night, as I said my prayers silently, I thought about all of the things that used to matter to me, the things I once asked Jesus for when I said my prayers, things like toys, friends, candy, for my family to be rich, and so on. Oh, how my priorities had changed?! Those things seemed so far away and so insignificant. Everything that truly mattered I had right there in that moment. I was safe. My mama and Tracy were safe. We were together. Most of all, I was building a relationship with God—the God that created the universe but knew me intimately and loved me just because I was His! Joy filled me from within. I smiled and let out a giggle. Mama wasn't asleep after all because, at that moment, she reached out her hand and brushed my hair away from my face with a tender and loving touch. Comforted by the warmth of her touch, I closed my eyes and was asleep before I knew it.

The days that followed my father's departure seemed ordinary in comparison to the experiences of my life thus far. After all of the trauma I witnessed, ordinary was a welcome gift.

We stayed in that little apartment for a while, and we were happy. It wasn't long before Mama decided it was time to move on with her life and start dating again. With that goal in mind, she filed for a divorce from my father.

Chapter 16

It is at this point in the story of my parents' relationship where I feel I must take you back to their beginning as opposed to moving forward in the tale of their ending.

As I mentioned previously, both were raised by loving Christian families. Both had examples of what it meant to genuinely live your life for God. Both were taught how to cleave to the path He set before them, and both were made vividly aware of the consequences that could take over your life if you walked away from Him.

That said, as most often do, my parents felt the need to put these lessons to the test. You see, they were also taught about God's love, His forgiveness, and His mercy. Each of them had heard the story of the prodigal son many times—how he took everything his father provided for him, left the safety and comfort of home, squandered all he'd been given, and ended up in a pigsty scrounging for food. It was in this moment of shame and regret the prodigal son realized even the servants in his father's house were provided for better than he, so he decided to return to his father and beg for a place among the servants. When his father sees him coming from far away, he runs to the son armed with his best robe, a ring, and shoes for his feet. In addition, the father commands the servants to prepare a feast in celebration of his son's return and start by killing the "fatted calf."

It was this parable of the unwavering, unconditional love of a father mirroring the love and grace of our heavenly Father that taught my parents about the power of redemption. They knew there was nothing they would or could do that would overshadow God's love for them. After all, He'd planned to send His only Son, Jesus, to die for our sins before the foundation of the world was ever set.

Confident this love was everlasting and the pathway to salvation would always be open, each of my parents ventured away from an intimate relationship with God in lieu of exploring the lures and lusts of sin.

When Mama was seventeen, she married for the first time with the hope of escaping her parents' authority. She was the second youngest of eight children, and she had a bit of a wild streak in her. She thought getting married was the answer that would allow her to live as freely and as wild as she desired. It wasn't. Huey was quite a few years older and an alcoholic who would often come home from a bender and beat her before passing out.

Still young and fearless, she decided to stand up to him.

One night, he came home even more intoxicated than usual and beat her worse than ever before passing out facedown in the middle of their bed. She sat in the corner of the bedroom crying, as she listened to the sounds coming from this man she'd come to loathe. She didn't need to look in order to know the sounds coming from him were snores accompanied by large quantities of drool and frothy slobber, not to mention the smell of beer intermingled with the distinctive smell of puke. No, this wasn't love she felt, but disgust.

Even at the beginning of their relationship, she had never loved Huey. He'd simply been the avenue she used to escape the rules her parents set. In this moment, she longed for those rules and the safety that accompanied them. All she wanted was to go home to her family, even if that meant taming her wild side. Right then, she realized she could go home. There was nothing stopping her. This time, she would not wait around for him to sleep off his stupor and apologize. She'd bought into those empty apologies and promises for the last time. As she thought about all of the times he'd hit her, pulled her hair, and kicked her after swearing to never do it again, the hurt she was feeling suddenly turned to anger and a need for retribution.

Mama knew Huey was what was referred to as a "blackout drunk." Once he passed out, it would be hours before anyone could rouse him. It was now her turn to give him a taste of his own medicine, of what she endured at his hands. She packed her meager belongings and loaded them into her car before returning to the bedroom where her husband still lay sleeping, unaware of what was about to take place. She started by stripping him naked and adding his clothes to the pile she'd already gathered by the door. She then tied his hands and feet to the bedposts with sheets making certain they were secure. She didn't want him to be able to get free from them should he awaken while she executed her plan. Confident his hands and feet were indeed secure, she proceeded to wet some towels and use them to beat Huey. With each strike, he writhed in agony and cried out in his sleep as if he were having a nightmare. Only, this was no dream. He would wake up to find this nightmare was a reality. She didn't stop until he was covered in welts. Mama wanted to make sure there would be bruising left to remind him of what she was capable of should he ever try to hurt her again. Satisfied the message would be evident, she picked up the pile of his clothes and walked outside where she soaked them in lighter fluid, set them on fire, and drove off.

Mama moved home to her parents' house and filed for a divorce from Huey. That would prove to be a more difficult task than she anticipated. It took more time to finalize the divorce than it did for their marriage to implode. In the meantime, Mama played by her own rules. She lived and acted as though she were a single woman free to do whatever she wanted.

Mama was never much of a drinker, but she loved to dance. It was her love of dance that often led her to nightclubs. Having grown up in a conservative Pentecostal home, the kind of dancing she liked to do was frowned upon. In her mind, those religious standards no longer seemed to matter. She'd been married and was now getting a divorce. She was an adult and free to do as she pleased.

It was in one of these nightclubs where she met my father. The year was 1971. Though her divorce was far from final, she was celebrating her liberation from Huey's grasp by going dancing with some friends. She could not have foreseen she was about to jump out of the frying pan and into the fire.

After all of the abuse Mama suffered at my father's hands, it never ceased to amaze me the way she lit up each time she told me the memory of how they met.

She remembered dancing all night to the point when her feet hurt so badly she could barely stand. Little did she know, the entire night she'd had an audience. The club's bouncer had been watching and admiring her as she danced. Now he noticed her rubbing her feet as she sat at a nearby table. Guessing she was in pain, he walked up, introduced himself, and offered to get her some aspirin from the office.

"Skip" was his name, and he was BEAUTIFUL! With his blond hair and piercing blue eyes, he could have easily been a descendant of Norse mythology, sent down from Odin himself. He spent the remainder of the night waiting on her, making her laugh and simply charming her. She was mesmerized by him. When it came time to leave, neither of them wanted to part, so he literally swept her up off her feet, put her over his shoulder, and carried her to his car. While doing so, he informed her friends he would be driving "His Judy" home.

After that night, they were inseparable. He was everything she dreamed of in a Prince Charming; handsome, strong, charismatic, protective, and best of all he only had eyes for her. There was no way she could let this Prince Charming slip through her hands, especially after the nightmare she'd lived through in her first relationship. This was no nightmare. This was different. This was a real-life fairytale. So hopelessly in love and certain it was the right thing to do, they moved in together despite the fact they were both still legally married.

Chapter 17

Shortly after my parents moved in together, my father was arrested. I have been told by those who knew him that he was sent to a Florida prison for permanently disfiguring a man's face in an unprovoked fight. The charges could have been anything from assault and battery to attempted murder. I do not know as they have since been expunged. What I do know is that the charges were serious enough to warrant a long, hard prison sentence.

As part of his punishment, Daddy was assigned to work on one of the last "chain gangs" in the country. Each day, he and some of his fellow inmates would be fastened to one another at the ankles with short lengths of chain that allowed just enough leeway to work side by side along the roadway in the hot Florida sun. Though the conditions were hard and, for some, unbearable, the men who worked on the chain gang were thankful just to be outside and away from the prison bars that confined them.

Always an opportunist, my father used bribes to convince the guards in charge of the chain gang to call Mama and let her know when and where they would be when they were outside working.

My mother's youngest sister, Martha Faye or Aunt Teeny as I know her, says that she remembers riding with Mama and Sue in an attempt to sneak a visit with my father while he was out on the chain gang one afternoon.

Aunt Teeny remembers him as striking. Working in the hot Florida sun for hours each day resulted in a golden tan to match his golden hair. Both seemed to enhance the blue of his eyes, adding to his movie-star features.

Still, no matter how handsome he was, the sight of him working, chained to other inmates in prison stripes on the side of the road, was enough to send a chill filled with fright to the very core of one's bones. Each prisoner held an average garden tool, a shovel, a hoe, or maybe just a rake. With the slightest of movement, any one of them could have easily become a deadly weapon.

Blinded by love and the thrill of stealing a kiss, Mama didn't care. She was willing to risk anything just to feel his touch for the briefest of moments.

According to Teeny, even her family loved him. How could they not? He lavished money on anyone around when he had it. He entranced all the girls with his good looks and Elvis vocals. He made the men feel a sense of brotherhood and camaraderie every man longs for. Daddy just seemed to have a way of capturing the room the moment he walked in and holding it hostage with his charms and mannerisms.

With certainty that he was her destiny, Mama waited for his release. It wasn't long. After less than a year in prison, Skip was released on parole, and at the end of 1972, they found themselves expecting their first child together, me. I was born in May of 1973.

Neither of them would obtain a final dissolution of marriage until May of 1976, three years after I was born.

With divorce decrees and a three-year-old version of me in tow, they made a public and legal declaration of their love for one another when they officially married for the FIRST time on June 6, 1976. That is right, FIRST TIME, but that is another marriage and another story.

While building their future together in this marriage, Daddy did what he could do better than anyone. He conned his way through life. Before long, my father was traveling all over the world, meeting celebrities and politicians, building a network of relationships and resources that would serve him throughout his life.

Meanwhile, he left my mother to care for me and get by as best as she could for long periods of time with little to no help from him. Still, she loved him. Despite all of the reasons she shouldn't, including his criminal history, his violent temper, even after the demonic episode that took place that night in the motel, she loved him, and thus she stayed.

Chapter 18

Disclaimer: I, in no way, endorse, condone, support, or encourage the purchase, ownership, reading, or looking at pornographic material of any kind. In fact, it contradicts my beliefs and my faith directly. However, my father provided me with a copy of one such magazine containing an article about his life when it was published as his way of bragging. I have used it for the sole purpose of validating the stories told to me by and about my father.

I've heard stories all of my life about my father and the things he has done. To be honest, even as his daughter, some of them have been hard to believe. When kids at school would ask who my father was and what he did for a living, I would simply tell them I didn't know because my parents were divorced. I was afraid that if I told them the truth, they wouldn't believe me. How could they when I had a hard time believing it myself? Though I knew bits and pieces of his stories, it wasn't until I read it, as an adult, for myself that I realized exactly who my father was.

Published in black and white, in, of all places, a pornographic magazine, there it was. There HE was! Penthouse Magazine, February 1995 edition. In the bottom left corner of the cover was the title of the article in all caps, "THE US VS. ROBERT VESCO: AN ASSASSIN'S ACCOUNT OF THE DESPERATE MANHUNT." Inside was an eight-page article written by the journalist Stuart Goldman. It was accompanied by an array of pictures taken by photographer Peter Liepke.

As I flipped through the pictures, I found no trace of the man my mother so often described as uncharacteristically handsome and debonair. Long gone were his good looks and golden locks. They'd been replaced with the battle scars left by a life lived hard and fast.

As I read the article, it was hard to believe it was about my father. It sounded more like something straight out of a crime fiction novel.

At the start of the interview, Daddy handed Stuart Goldman one of his business cards. It boasted—bars emptied, wars fought, revolutions started, governments run, unions organized, and insurance collected.

Those claims did not begin to encompass all that he was or would be. He had experience as a bounty hunter, bodyguard, drug smuggler, counterfeit money smuggler, and launderer. He'd brought bail jumpers back across the Mexican-American border in the trunk of his car.

There wasn't much James "Skip" Wilkins did not do. Say what you want about the man or the many horrible things that he did, but there is no denying he lived anything but a boring, mediocre life.

On the contrary, it was a life filled with excitement, intrigue, and, many times, danger.

He once lived as a roommate with a famous wrestler while working to promote concerts and wrestling matches. He earned his pilot's license so he could fly airplanes. He even served as captain on several ships.

Whether he was a pimp or the president of a religious mission for the homeless, you never knew where he would be from one day to the next or what he would be doing.

Adventure seemed to be his middle name. He trapped alligators in Florida lakes, rivers, and swamps with my Uncle Bob. He delivered babies and once played piano in a local country band and worked as an all-night Deejay for the famous broadcast radio station, Q105.

It seemed my daddy had ties to everyone, from the mafia bosses and drug lords to US district attorneys. His relationships were far reaching on both sides of the law. Those connections made it possible for him to go anywhere and be anyone at the drop of a hat and with no notice.

The people he knew and associated with ranged from convicts to celebrities. He had the personal and private phone numbers to actors, former Costa Rican presidents, as well as countless others including televangelists, madams, senators, congressmen, pro golfers, informants, prize fighters, law enforcement authorities, and many, many others.

He was quoted as saying that his little black book was his most prized possession.

His adventures would carry him to the craziest of places.

In the 1970s, he appeared as a contestant on *The Price Is Right* where he won several household furniture items and sold them before he ever got home from the show.

He would go on to further his wanderlust with many more conquests including work with the television news magazine show, *A Current Affair*, where he helped cover the case involving the Menendez brothers who were convicted of killing their parents.

Throughout his life, Daddy's thirst for adventure never seemed to be quenched. Nothing could satisfy the need to chase his next big thrill. I suppose it is that thirst that nearly cost him his life many times.

In 1972, during a visit to Costa Rica, in which he went to rob graves of jewels and other valuables customarily buried with the dead, he met a young woman named Abbie and married her on a whim. Shortly after he learned she was pregnant, coincidentally at the same time, my mother was pregnant with me.

My half-sister Jennifer was born in late 1973, just months after my birth. The marriage to Abbie was never legal as Daddy was already married to his first wife, Linda, and engaged to my mama here in the United States. Nevertheless, my father purchased a ranch in Costa Rica where Abbie and Jennifer lived and where he would visit them often. As a result, by 1976, Costa Rica had become a second home to Daddy.

The interview in Penthouse primarily focuses on Daddy's life in 1976, the same year he and my mother were married. He was on parole from prison and not allowed to travel outside of the United States.

It was during this time that he was working as a concert promoter, which required him to travel. Never one to play by the rules, Daddy flew to Costa Rica as he'd done many times before to set up and promote a concert in San Jose.

Daddy was in Costa Rica booking rock bands for a place called Cariari Country Club. While there, my father heard that one of the United States' most wanted men, Robert Vesco, was working out of an office nearby. Robert Vesco was wanted for absconding with nearly $250 million of investor funds, causing his rise to the top of the most wanted list of several government agencies, including the SEC, CIA, FBI, DEA, IRS, and the US Customs Department.

Curiosity and, I'm sure, a little greed set in, and Daddy could not help himself. He had to meet this man who'd accomplished what Daddy only dared aspire to—the ultimate con. To say that Daddy wasn't scared of anything would be an understatement of epic proportions. Even when he should have been scared, he wasn't. Without hesitation, he walked right into the building where Vesco's office was housed in downtown San Jose and asked for a meeting.

Of course, he did not get what he asked for. Robert Vesco was a wanted man, and they would be crazy to let just anyone off the street in to see him. Instead, they sent out Alberto Abreu. He was Vesco's right hand, and the litmus test one must pass prior to meeting Vesco. He would determine if Daddy passed the test or not.

Daddy was as smooth a talker as there ever was. His skills did not disappoint Alberto Abreu. My father told him all of the ways in which he would be an asset to the organization. He had his master's license that allowed him to captain ships. He also had a pilot's license that enabled him to fly small aircraft. There were his ties to the mafia, celebrities, and various people in positions of authority that might prove useful. It did not take long for Daddy to talk his way into a job as the captain of Robert Vesco's yacht, The Patricia.

Once he was given the job, he explained that he would need a few months before he could start. He had obligations back home in

Florida that needed to be taken care of. Those obligations were my mama and me.

Upon his return to the United States, Daddy was taken away by the US Marshals to One Foley Square in New York under the pretense he had been subpoenaed to appear before a grand jury, which never happened. It became apparent that the US government had Vesco's organization under surveillance. Though they could not extradite him, they kept a close eye on everyone who visited Vesco's San Jose offices. Having seen my daddy on one of those surveillance missions, he now found himself in New York meeting with attorneys from the various agencies who wanted Vesco.

Spearheading these meetings was a man by the name of Robert Fiske Jr. He was a US attorney at the time and had previously worked on the Watergate investigation.

During the course of these meetings, it became clear to Daddy he was being recruited to spy on Robert Vesco. They used his parole as leverage to make him do their bidding. Traveling outside of the United States was grounds for revocation, which would send him back to prison for the remainder of his sentence. He was told to go to work for Vesco's organization as planned, infiltrate the inner circle by getting as close to Vesco as possible, and report back to the US Attorney Fiske everything he found out. According to the article, Daddy was even asked whether or not he would be willing to assassinate or kidnap Robert Vesco. If not, they wanted to know if he knew someone who would. Daddy assured them that he was willing to do whatever they wanted him to do. In exchange, they agreed not to violate his parole, and in addition, they would expunge his record and set up witness protection for his family. He was in.

Chapter 19

Following his meeting with US officials, Daddy returned to Costa Rica with the intention of completing the mission to spy on Robert Vesco, report his findings, and, if necessary, kidnap or even kill Vesco at the direction of Attorney Fiske and the US government.

To say that things did not go according to the plan would be a gross understatement. When Daddy arrived in Costa Rica, he called Vesco's secretary. She directed Daddy to a hotel where he would be picked up. He went to the hotel as instructed, and after several hours, a car pulled up, and my father got in. The driver started out for San Jose, though instead of the usual, direct route, he took a route that led through the sketchiest parts of San Jose. Daddy started to get a little nervous when the driver pulled up to a disco club located in a notoriously bad area of town. The driver parked the car, and they waited.

Before long, a Jeep parked behind them, carrying three large men who got out and walked up to the car Daddy was in. They instructed him to get out. He did. They frisked him. Content he wasn't armed or wired, they motioned for another car to approach. It was a gray Mercedes. The car stopped, and the men told my father to get in the front passenger seat.

As soon as he was in the car, he realized that Robert Vesco was sitting in the backseat. Finally, the man my father had been wanting to meet for some time was no more than two feet from him. Daddy introduced himself as Johnny Turner, not wanting to reveal his real name. With this lie, my father and Vesco commenced with their dangerous game of chess as the driver drove them around the streets of San Jose. At one point, Vesco said, "Mr. Wilkins, look, let's stop the game." That is when Daddy knew things were about to change. Vesco advised Daddy that he knew who he was and what his connections were to the US government all along. He was also aware of the meetings he attended in New York in which my father was recruited to spy for US officials.

Vesco then revealed to my father all sorts of information the US agencies could have used against him, including where the money he embezzled was located, along with the fact that he had the support of a US president. He was referring to Richard Nixon, a relationship built on the fact that Vesco made a rather large and illegal campaign contribution to help insure Nixon's election.

The conversation continued and seemed to turn in my father's favor when Vesco asked if he would like to work for him. Without hesitation, Daddy accepted the offer. This was Robert Vesco's territory. There was no way he was going to refuse an offer when that refusal would most likely result in his death.

After agreeing to work for Vesco, he was taken back to his hotel and instructed to be ready for someone to pick him up early the next morning. Sure enough, there was a knock on his door, and he opened it to find a large, intimidating man armed with a P57. Something was definitely off.

Hesitantly, Daddy got into the car with the armed man who drove directly to the Russian Embassy. He ushered my father to the second floor where Robert Vesco was waiting. He was not the kind, friendly man from the day before. No, this time, he handed my father a script and demanded he call his contact in the US Attorney's office and read it. After looking at the script, Daddy realized they were trying to make him give false intel to the United States. He tried telling them that if he read the script, the United States would know something was wrong. He explained to them that there were code words set up ahead of time to be used in place of actual names for various people and places. For instance, Robert Vesco would only ever be referred to as Vickie.

Vesco was unmoved in his stance and was adamant that Daddy do as he demanded. He forced my father to make the call and read the script as it was written.

Once Daddy finished reading the script, Vesco hung up the phone and left the room.

Daddy was taken back to his hotel and told to stay there. Someone would come to pick him up the next morning.

In the middle of the night, the hotel room door was knocked down. In walked several guys wearing uniforms and armed with automatic weapons. They told Daddy that there was an immigration warrant for his arrest and he must go with them to the immigration office.

Outside of the hotel, they forced him into a truck that had a covered back without windows so he was unable to see where they were taking him. When the truck finally stopped, they were not at the immigration office. They were at the old San Jose penitentiary.

Daddy was thrown into a cell and locked up.

He described the cell as being more like a dungeon or a cave. He would later learn the place was actually referred to as La Cave by the locals.

There were no lights, no sink, not even a toilet, nothing.

The floor was covered in feces and urine.

During the first couple of days, Daddy remembered being given bread and water, but those days were followed by beatings and interrogations.

When Daddy failed to produce the information they desired from him, he was given pills to induce a state of delirium in hopes he would cooperate with their demands.

They wanted him to sign a confession that stated he was sent by the US government to assassinate Robert Vesco.

There was nothing about infiltrating his organization or even kidnapping, just the order to assassinate. Daddy was certain had he signed the confession, they would have killed him.

As each day passed and their efforts to make my father sign a confession failed, their desperation grew more intense. Finally, they showed him a picture of me that they found in his wallet.

I was not quite two in the picture. Daddy said he cried as he stared at the picture while they told him he would never see me again if he did not sign the confession. Feeling like they had finally broken him, they left him alone in his cell to consider his options.

Meanwhile, there was a man in the cell next to him. The soldiers took the man out of his cell and led him to the courtyard.

My father said he heard the sound of guns ringing through the air, and he knew they were firing at the man who had been his neighbor just moments before.

The next morning, the soldiers returned, only this time it was for my daddy. Without saying a word, they blindfolded him, grabbed him up under his armpits, stood him on his feet, and dragged him to the courtyard. Once in the courtyard, they tied him to a chair and removed the blindfold.

My father looked around to find he was sitting in front of a brick wall covered in bullet holes and blood stains. The man in charge, known to Daddy as the "General," shoved the written confession in front of his face and asked, "Are you ready to sign?" Daddy thought about the picture of me, of my mama, and of what he was certain happened to the man in the next cell. He signed the confession.

Chapter 20

The incident in San Jose would lead to a life-long friendship between Robert Vesco and my father. It was a relationship that served both of them very well. It kept Vesco one step ahead of those who sought his arrest, and it kept my father from death and/or imprisonment more times throughout his life than he cared to remember.

As unbelievable as this story sounds, it is one of many, many, many unbelievable stories that happen to be my father's truths, and maybe I will explore those with you at a later time, in another book.

That is because it is at this point in the story that I want to tell you about two contrasting paths, two contrasting ends, two very contrasting choices made.

Jump ahead in time with me if you will to the year 2001. Much time has passed, and many changes have taken place in my life, again part of another story for another time.

Suffice it to say, I am married for the third time and am the mother of three beautiful, amazing children.

We've recently moved to Alabama from Florida and are just settling in.

My phone rings in the middle of the night. It is my brother calling to notify me that my father has died.

Though I love him very much, I haven't spoken with my daddy in many years because of the lifestyle he lives and the people he associates with.

With all my flaws and imperfections, I am doing everything I can to raise my children with a foundation built on a loving relationship with God as I attempt to keep them safe from any known danger, including my father.

According to what I have been told, my father accidentally overdosed.

My father lived most of his adult life as a functioning drug addict and alcoholic. As he aged and the rough life he lived started to catch up with him, it became hard for him to get around, which made it difficult to procure the drugs he wanted.

Several years prior to his passing, through con and manipulation, Daddy convinced the VA doctors to implant a self-administering morphine port into his wrist. Because of the "self-administered" status, there were times when he would give himself a shot of morphine, pass out, wake up fifteen to twenty minutes later, and shoot another dose because he'd forgotten about the last one he'd given himself. Soon he was mixing the morphine with copious amounts of whiskey. When the two were no longer enough to take him into the blissful abyss he sought, Daddy added crack cocaine into the mix.

According to my brother, Terry, the day before my father passed away, he picked him up from the hospital following a brief admission for some health-related issue.

Daddy had nowhere to go, so Terry took him home with him. Once he got Daddy settled in and comfortable, Terry went to bed and left Daddy in a recliner, watching television.

The next morning, Terry woke up, went to the kitchen, and made a pot of coffee. He called out to my father to ask if he wanted a cup, but he didn't answer. Terry walked over to the recliner where he found my father dead.

While my brother was sleeping, in the middle of the night, Daddy smoked crack cocaine, chased it with a glass of whiskey, and then gave himself a boost of morphine.

It killed him.

I didn't cry—at least not then. It would be several years before I cried over my father's passing. I couldn't even bring myself to attend his memorial service.

I knew how much Papa Wilkins loved his son, my daddy. I also knew that he wanted, even needed, to believe that my father made things right with God before he drew his last breath and that he was now, finally, at peace in heaven with Nana who had gone before him years prior.

I could not simply accept that narrative as fact. I am well aware that God is loving, forgiving, and restorative, just as the father in the parable of the Prodigal Son, even more so. However, my father did everything he could to mock God and take advantage of His people at every opportunity he had. Many times, I watched Nana and Papa beg him to give his life to God, to turn his life around and fall into the open, waiting arms of the Father who so desperately chased after him. No amount of pleading moved him to respond with anything other than disdain that they would dare ask.

I hung up the phone after speaking with my brother, and I prayed. I needed an answer from God. I needed to know if there was a chance my daddy had cried out to Him as death came.

He answered me.

When I closed my eyes that night, I had a dream. I don't often dream, but that night, I did.

I was standing inside a small house located at the south end of a cemetery. A friend of mine was there, and she was speaking to me though I could not hear what she was saying due to the classical music that was playing in the background. The door to the house was open, and I could see past my friend out into the cemetery. There was a coffin that had not yet been lowered into the ground, and it was open. I could see my daddy in the coffin. He was alive, sitting up, smiling, and waving for me to come toward him. I could also see a minister, dressed like the minister from the show "Little House on the Prairie," and he was walking toward the coffin from the west side. I did not respond to Daddy as he beckoned for me to come close because it didn't seem right. All of a sudden, in the midst of smiling and waving, he pulled out a gun. He shot the minister, shot at me, and then shot himself.

I woke up!

Though I felt I knew exactly what the dream meant, I wanted confirmation. I immediately called a trusted friend who is a minister and a devout man of God. I wanted his interpretation of what the dream meant.

He confirmed what I already knew.

The dream was a revelation that my father did not make it to heaven, no matter how badly I or anyone else wanted that to be true. My friend went on to give me further interpretation.

In my dream, the minister represented God and the Body of Christ as a whole. I was a representation of my father's family. The act of smiling and waving in an attempt to draw the minister and myself closer to him before taking his own life and attempting to take ours said that Daddy was playing games with all of us right up until the very end.

It broke my heart. This was my father, my daddy, the man I once cherished above all others.

Yet, as I said, it took me years to cry. Even then, it wasn't because of his death.

I remember it clearly, we'd moved back to Florida. It was Father's Day, and I'd just left visiting my stepfather. We were riding down the interstate, listening to old fifties and sixties music when THE song came on, "Don't know much about history. Don't know Biology. All I know is that I love you…" The dam broke. All the lost years of father and daughter moments, all the laughs left silent, all the possibilities of what could have been, most of all, the knowledge that I will never see him again. Not here. Not in eternity. I will never see my daddy again. He is lost forever.

Chapter 21

As I stated before, I want to tell you an ending in drastic contrast to that of my father. To do so, let's jump ahead through many years of my mother's life to the time of her passing. Again, there have been many twists and turns all of which have led to a long, intimate, and unwavering relationship with Jesus worthy of her own book. For now, I am going to tell you about her passing with the hope of imparting to you a peace that can be had even in the face of death, when you have returned to the waiting arms of God somewhere along the path you take in life.

For several years, my mama and her last husband, David, lived in an assisted living facility, following their retirement from Pastoring. Mama fell and tore her meniscus, leaving her unable to walk for several months, which resulted in her being placed in a rehabilitative facility with the hopes of regaining her mobility. In December of 2020 while in physical rehab, she contracted an upper respiratory infection, which was exacerbated by the COPD she suffered from due to her years as a cosmetologist. When antibiotics did not seem to be helping her, the nurses decided to send her to the hospital via ambulance. Upon her arrival, she was found to have pneumonia in both of her lungs. She was immediately put on oxygen and antibiotics. When neither helped, she was placed on a BiPap machine and advised she needed to be intubated. Mama refused the intubation because of a bad experience she'd had in years past that almost killed her.

Mama was told that without the intubation, she would die, and so she chose to die.

With her faculties in full function and her mind as clear as ever, she chose to die.

With confidence in her destination, she chose to die.

It would be a few days before they removed the BiPap and all other life-sustaining means, allowing her time to say goodbye to her loved ones. With each moment that passed and every conversation she had, she seemed to grow more and more excited.

When asked why she was so joyful and full of excitement, she said, "I finally get to go home and see my Jesus!"

She knew what her future held. For that matter, she knew she had a future! She'd spent all of her later years in love with and surrendered to God and His plan for her life.

In her final moments, with her children and grandchildren at her bedside, she held my hand and wiped the tears from my eyes as I told her how much I loved her and assured her that I would see her again. Then, at her request, we sang to her, "Peace, peace…wonderful peace, coming down from the Father above…sweep over my spirit forever, I pray…in fathomless billows of love."

She smiled and closed her eyes.

She was home.

Epilogue

Looking back over my life, I can see how the things I experienced as a child took a much bigger toll on my life than I even realized. It wasn't until I started writing my story that I discovered how high and wide the wall was that I built around these memories. I thought that I was protecting myself, believing those episodes of trauma did not define me or change who I was meant to be in any way.

I was so very wrong. With each brick I tear down, I discover how very real my struggle is.

I always thought of myself as a kind, loving, and caring person. I used to be accused of "wearing my feelings on my sleeve."

As it turns out, my self-examination could not have been further from the truth.

You see, deep inside of me is a part of him—a part of my daddy, Skip. No matter how badly I want to carve it out and pretend it never existed, IT DOES! Although I gave my life to God a very long time ago, in the process of trying to become everything He wants me to be, I am finding that with every brick I tear down, He allows me to see something within myself that does not reflect His characteristics.

Every day, I am faced with a choice of whether or not I will be the person my DNA and life experiences dictate or if I will take on the characteristics my heavenly Father says I can have. Some days, the choice is easy. When life gives you rainbows and butterflies, it is easy to reflect the nature of the God of creation.

Then there are other days—days when you are hurting—and it seems that the hurt will never end. All you want to do is lash out in response. It is at those times when I can hear Skip's voice in my head, telling me to never be the one on the receiving side of pain. I can see his eyes burning through me, willing me to react the way he would. The ideas of revenge that fester are as innumerable as they are uniquely spiteful. The idea of forgiveness doesn't even begin to enter into the equation unless I make the choice to deny my flesh, deny my sinful nature, or deny that ache for retribution.

I can tell you this conscious choice making has not been easy, to say the least, yet I am learning that true love does not keep a record of wrong, it is quick to forgive, and it restores that that is seemingly irreparably broken.

That is the Father I choose to emulate—the Father who loved me so much that He looked ahead in time and saw me while I was yet a sinner and chose to die for me because He knew that I was in need of a savior. He knew that I would be the daughter of a man who would do unspeakable things. He knew that I would also hurt people just as I had been hurt. He knew that I would fail people just as I was failed.

I would fail as a daughter, a mother, a wife, and a friend. I never intended to fail. It was always my goal to be the best at everything I ever attempted, but that has not been the reality of my life.

That said, I am so very grateful that He put something inside of me that caused my surrender when He called me. I am so very thankful that the same ingredient causes me to long for a closer relationship with Him every day.

I choose to forgive because I have been forgiven. I choose mercy because without mercy, my debts would be impossible to repay. I choose grace because the grace I have been given covers my multitude of sins.

I will never know why my earthly father never surrendered to the love, forgiveness, mercy, or grace that was freely given to all, but I do know that I have made my choice. I only pray that those I have wronged will forgive me and know that I am still a work in progress and my love for them is unwavering along with my determination to continue to become more like my heavenly Father and less like my earthly one.

About the Author

Born in Tampa, Florida, to James Wilkins and Judy Lee, Angela Peacock was raised in the small town of Plant City, Florida. Living in Plant City played a big part in shaping the person Angela is today. Her love of fishing, exploring dirt roads, reading a book under the shade of a grandfather oak tree, and taking naps after church on Sunday can be attributed to the slow-paced life of the little town she grew up in—a place where everyone seems to know everyone and they all love and revere God and country.

Angela always felt called to write. It was as if God was pouring into her soul and out through her fingertips every time she put pen to paper. Yet it wasn't until now, after two failed marriages and a third being weighed in the balance, after the death of her mother, when her relationship with her children is strained and seemingly irreparable, when she is finally, solely dependent on Jehovah, that she has stepped into and embraced her calling to write. May this book bless you as it has blessed Angela in writing it and tearing down her walls brick by brick with every word.